Forgiveness

J I M
G R A H A M

Scripture Union
130 City Road, London EC1V 2NJ

First published 1991

British Library CIP Data
Graham, Jim
  Forgiveness.
  1. Christian life. Forgiveness
  I. Title
  248.4
  ISBN 0 86201 509 X

Acknowledgements

The prayer of St Francis quoted in chapter 1 is copyright © 1967, Franciscan Communications, Los Angeles, CA 90015. Reprinted with permission. The quotation from *Sit, Walk, Stand,* by Watchman Nee, in chapter 4, is copyright © Angus I Kinnear. The book is published by Kingsway. *Tramp for the Lord*, by Corrie ten Boom (an extract from which is used in chapter 4) is published in the UK and Commonwealth by CLC. 'As we are gathered', quoted in chapter 7, is by J Daniels and is copyright © 1979 Word (UK) Ltd. The quotation with which chapter 7 closes is from *The Alternative Service Book 1980* copyright © 1980 the Central Board of France of the Church of England. 'You laid aside your majesty', quoted in chapter 8, is by Noel Richards and is copyright © 1985 Thankyou Music, PO Box 75, Eastbourne, East Sussex BN23 6NW, UK. It is used by permission. 'Thank you, O my Father', quoted in chapter 8, is by Melody Green and is copyright © Birdwing Music/ Cherry Lane Music.

All Bible quotations, except where otherwise stated, are from The Good News Bible – Old Testament: Copyright © American Bible Society 1976; New Testament: Copyright © American Bible Society 1966, 1971, 1976.

Phototypeset by Input Typesetting Ltd, London.
Printed and bound in Great Britain by
Cox and Wyman Ltd, Reading.

Contents

Preface

'Forgiveness is the key which unlocks the door of resentment and the handcuffs of hatred. It breaks the chains of bitterness and the shackles of selfishness. The forgiveness of Jesus not only takes away our sins, it makes them as if they had never been.' So wrote Corrie ten Boom out of her long experience of walking with God and ministering in the name of Jesus. Not only do we need to be forgiven, but we need to forgive. Each is deeply related to the other. So fundamental is this to the Christian life that when Jesus commented on the Lord's Prayer (which we should really call 'the disciples' prayer'!), he commented only on forgiveness.

A relationship with God is impossible if we are unable to receive his forgiveness; and our relationship with others is disastrously impaired if we are unable to release them in forgiveness. There is no real way to get our world back together again except as each of us begins – with ourselves and with those to whom we immediately relate – to explore forgiveness.

The Collins English Dictionary defines forgiveness as 'the act of forgiving, or the state of being forgiven.' It speaks of the word 'forgive' as meaning 'ceasing to blame or hold resentment against (someone or something). To grant a pardon for (a mistake, wrongdoing, etc.). To free or pardon (someone) from penalty.' That is what this book is about. I have written no book which has so affected my own personal life quite as much as this one, as I have tried to work out the realities of what I have written in my own life.

Jim Graham

1

Shake hands and go home!

My recollections of my junior school days are pleasant enough, by and large. Each day was much like the previous one and the day after. From time to time, however, the relative calm was disturbed by two boys (not always the same two boys!) falling out. Tempers flared up over some issue, but fighting on school premises was a punishable offence – and I remember one headmaster well able to implement the penalty. On one occasion a row occurred at the morning break and only the 'lookout' of the staffroom windows prevented blows being struck there and then. In spite of great encouragement from the gathering crowd of rival supporters, verbal viciousness was as far as it went. It continued, unusually, throughout the day, and word went round like wildfire that the matter was to be settled completely after school hours in a more appropriate manner behind the cinema, on a large vacant piece of ground about three hundred yards away from the school gates.

The crowd duly gathered and the two rival groups appeared, each with their angered gladiator. Jackets and jerseys were removed and battle commenced. None of us had ever heard of the Marquis of Queensbury and his boxing rules and few, if any, knew what the quarrel was about anyway.

The fierce battle between the two boys was short-lived as a teacher appeared on the scene. Everyone was awe-struck. What would he do? Would he do anything, or simply refer the matter to a higher authority? Would he call the police? No one had the slightest idea – least of all the two combatants, now strangely passive. He walked straight up to them and to everyone's astonishment he demanded they shake hands and go home. It was all so British; such a let-down; so unsatisfactory. They not only shook hands (two scruffy little boys!) but they went home – together!

Relationships are really of the stuff of life, but they can be very vulnerable and fragile. A word, an act, an attitude – sometimes even a look – can fracture a relationship quickly. Coldness, suspicion, animosity, resentment, hurt and bitterness can result. The passage of time only tends to emphasise the damage that has been done. Yet we cannot avoid one another, we need to relate to one another, even if the best we can manage is hurtful disinterest or blatant hostility. Good relationships are clearly preferable but can seem unattainable.

Michael Christopher wrote a powerful play, *The Black Angel*, in which he explored with considerable pathos the issue of forgiveness. Those who have seen or read it are normally left haunted with the most painful question – short of our own death – the question of forgiveness. What do we do when we forgive someone? What actually happens between two people when one forgives and the other is forgiven? Why does it take a miracle to pull it off? Is this really what happened to the two little boys whom I described earlier or did they simply, because of circumstances, let the matter drop in an unsatisfactory and unresolved way? Is that what forgiveness really is?

The Black Angel is about a former German army general called Engel, who tried to make a new beginning for his wife and himself outside a little French village after World War II was over. He had been in prison for thirty years – sentenced at the War Crimes Court at Nuremberg in 1946. Now incognito, he hoped, he was building a cabin in the mountains. His past was behind him – paid for by three lost decades in prison. His dominating concern was to forget the past and build what remained of his future.

However, a French journalist named Morrieu could not forget. His whole family had been brutally massacred in a village Engel's army had overrun during the early days of the war. Every person in that village had been executed by Engel's soldiers. For thirty long years Morrieu had waited with bitterness and resentment deepening and increasing, and planned to have his revenge and to bring justice, as he saw it. Now the time had come – his waiting was over and his research accurate and complete. He went into the village and planted hatred and fear in the minds and hearts of the people. He achieved what he set out to do, and they planned to go up the mountain, burn the cabin down, and assassinate the former general.

However, Morrieu had some lingering questions, and he needed answers which only Engel could give. So he went to Engel's cabin on the afternoon before the night of vengeance. He introduced himself to the shaken Engel and spent the whole afternoon in a terrible inquisition of the now old man. He was driven to get the whole wretched story straight before Engel died with his secrets. Unexpectedly, and devastatingly, as the afternoon wore on, revenge began to taste sour in Morrieu's mouth. After these thirty long years of waiting and burning and fostering hatred, for the first time Morrieu had doubts. In plunging himself into Engel's soul he tore his own soul to pieces. Left with no alternative, Morrieu warned Engel of the villagers' attack that coming night – and offered to take him to safety!!

The general waited a long, interminable minute before responding to Morrieu's offer of rescue. At last he replied that he would accept Morrieu's offer on one condition –

that Morrieu would forgive him! But Morrieu could not do that. He could save him, but he could not forgive him.

The villagers came as an undisciplined mob and burned the cabin to the ground and mercilessly shot Engel and his wife.

What was it that Engel wanted more than life itself? What was it in the deep places of his being that he needed so badly that he would rather die than live without it? What was the one thing that Morrieu did not have the power to give without losing his integrity? What is this miracle called forgiveness? Surely it is much deeper and more fundamental than simply shaking hands and going home as if nothing had ever happened?

What forgiveness isn't

Often our understanding is helped when we consider what something is not. It clears the ground and the negatives often sharpen our appreciation of the positive.

Forgiveness is not a feeling. The Bible never confuses forgiveness with feelings – neither in giving nor in receiving forgiveness. Often we hear someone say, 'I can never forgive him for that!' The implication is, 'I do not *feel* I can ever forgive him!' We need to introduce a spiritual rule into our thinking that will have a staggering effect upon our practice. Instead of saying, 'I cannot!' I need to substitute, 'I will not!' or, 'I have not learned how to yet!' Forgiveness is a decision not an emotion – it operates in the area of the will rather than the area of the feelings. The thrilling reality of the matter is that as I will to choose God's way, the Holy Spirit comes alongside me to enable me to walk in God's way. Astonishingly, what has been devoid of feeling can be filled with it as we walk in the decisions we have made and exercise our will, enjoying the reality of the Holy Spirit's enabling.

Forgiveness is not forgetting. How many of us have stumbled here. The little phrase, 'forgive and forget', has tied these two too closely together and we have concluded that one is invalid without the other – if I cannot forget, I have not forgiven. This is not so! Forgiveness *is* possible without forgetting. It is a psychological fact of life that nothing that happens to us is ever really forgotten. The passage of the years may soften or dull the memory, and the details (particularly if they have caused us pain) may become somewhat blurred, but even when we have difficulty in recalling some event or circumstance it has sunk into our subconscious mind. It is not really forgotten: astonishingly, after a lifetime of not remembering, a childhood memory can suddenly startle us with its momentary vividness. Such is the reality of the situation, and we need to settle for that.

When we forgive, all the details may live on in our memory – but the bitterness and hurt and resentment which surround these details are siphoned off. In practical terms, we can still remember the event, but emotionally and spiritually it no longer affects us. It is true that God can forgive *and* forget, but we cannot.

I was deeply impressed by a story I heard of a lady who gave a strong impression to all around that she had a 'hot line' to God. This somewhat irritated rather than impressed a bishop who was present at a conference where the lady was a delegate. In conversation with her one day he said, 'Yesterday I confessed three sins to God. If you are as able, as you say you are, to hear what God says, ask him what these three sins were. I told him about them in my confession.' The lady agreed without hesitation to do just that, and asked for twenty-four hours to conduct her enquiry. On the next day the bishop asked her if she had asked God about his three confessed sins. She said that she had. 'What did he say? Did he tell you what they were?' the bishop asked. She said in reply, 'He told me he couldn't remember what they were since you had confessed them and received forgiveness and cleansing for them.' God has a wonderful facility for forgetting those things which we have confessed and which he has forgiven.

Forgiveness is not pretending. Pretence is immature and unreal. To be a Christian is not to enter into some kind of fantasy land where we can escape some of the harsher and more painful realities of life. Christianity is not cheap escapism. As Christians we are compelled to face realities about ourselves, God, others, and the world around, and still have a living hope. Some, however, can only deal with an offence by pretending that it never happened. Wishing that it had never happened does not alter the fact that it did happen, damage has been done, and wounds have been inflicted, either by us or upon us.

Forgiveness is clear, logical action which faces reality – however painful, wounding, humiliating, or disillusioning. It is an act of the will which says to the thoughts and feelings and reactions that result from that hurt: 'The matter is now over – I forgive in Jesus' name.'

Forgiveness is not recalling. Long ago when writing to that remarkable and yet woefully fragmented church in the rich and populous city of Corinth, the apostle Paul said that love does not store up the memory of any wrong it has received. The word which is translated 'keep' or 'store up' (*logizesthai*) is an accountant's word. It is a word which is used for entering an item in a ledger so that it will not be forgotten. That is precisely what many people do with the slights and hurts and disappointments they have received – they store them up; write them down in the ledgers of their minds; ensure that they will be neither overlooked not forgotten; record clearly every detail of words spoken and deeds done. It is one thing to be unable to forget, but it is quite another to ensure that we remember. So many people nurse their wrath to keep it warm; they brood over their wrongs until it is impossible to forget them.

The past is very real, but it is dead and anything which keeps the wrongs of the past alive needs to be ceremonially (perhaps), but unceremoniously destroyed. The letter received; the gradually fading photograph; the article that constantly haunts the memory – get rid of them.

Burn them, bury them, destroy them one way or another. They serve no good purpose now except to awaken the memory of an incident, an event, a relationship, a phase of life that has gone forever, and must no longer affect the present.

Forgiveness is not demanding that, before we will forgive them, the person who caused grief and did wrong must change. So often we demand that others attempt to earn our forgiveness of them. Unconditional forgiveness is vital. More than that; many times we need to start with an apology for our part in the upset. How human and understandable is the conversation which includes comments like: 'I was wrong, but so were you!' 'I'm sorry, but you must realise that it was not all my fault!' 'If I am wrong then I apologise!' 'I'm quite willing to say I am sorry if you want me to!' In all of these statements there is a certain lack of conviction about my share of responsibility for what has happened. They show an appreciation that all is not well, but imply that I am not quite to blame.

It takes humility to say honestly 'I am wrong', in an unqualified way. Forgiveness is always self-giving without self-seeking. Many years ago someone said in my hearing: 'You need never lose your peace over someone else's sin.' I have not always learned that lesson, but I have a faithful partner who constantly reminds me of it.

Long ago St Francis prayed a prayer that often expresses the need of my own heart:

Make me a channel of your peace.
Where there is hatred let me bring your love;
where there is injury, your pardon, Lord;
and where there's doubt, true faith in you.
Make me a channel of your peace.
Where there's despair in life let me bring hope;
where there is darkness, only light;
and where there's sadness, ever joy.
Make me a channel of your peace.
It is in pardoning that we are pardoned,

in giving to all men that we receive;
and in dying that we're born to eternal life.
Oh, master, grant that I may never seek
so much to be consoled as to console;
to be understood as to understand;
to be loved, as to love with all my soul.

Forgiveness is not so much demanding that my needs are met and my position and posture vindicated and secured, as it is desiring that there would be nothing in my heart that would be unacceptable before God and a hindrance to others entering into all that God has for them. Forgiveness is my unconditional releasing of another or others so that they can be free to become all that God has in mind for them.

It is misleading to say that time heals – only forgiveness does that!

What forgiveness is

Forgiveness starts with the way in which God brings sinful people into a right relationship with himself. It is an act of grace, that is, of undeserved favour, of sheer unconditional generosity, on the basis of the work of God in Jesus Christ, and is offered to the repentant sinner who trusts God's promise. Any understanding of forgiveness must begin, not with our liberal-mindedness, but with God and his love. In the Bible this is seen most clearly in the writings of the apostle Paul. He explains the significance of what Jesus the Messiah did: it makes possible the forgiveness of the sinner who responds in faith to the revelation of God in Jesus Christ. There are two main parts to Paul's declaration of this thrilling and amazing reality.

We're in a mess
From his own experience as a Jew committed to fulfilling the law of God, Paul discovered that, try as he might, in the end the law always condemned him. No matter what

he did he could never be really free from guilt. And Christ does not abolish the law, if anything he reveals its true implication – the total devotion of our whole being to God. So man is unable to assume that he can earn acceptance with God, but is confronted with the devastating fact that the law of God condemns him, and that he is totally impotent to rescue himself from this plight. Unless help comes to him from somewhere outside himself he is doomed to despair.

We can be forgiven

The second element in Paul's teaching is about the righteousness of God. This involves not only the righteousness which God requires of everyone, but also the activity by which he can make sinful people righteous – his forgiveness of those who are prepared to be joined to him. Paul declares with penetrating clarity and awesome simplicity that our hope lies in the perfect righteousness of the life of Jesus Christ. Men may be critical of his conduct and fail to grasp his teaching, but neither friend nor foe could ever realistically condemn his character. But Jesus doesn't just show us, by his holy life, that God is righteous: by his death he makes it possible for us to be righteous too. The righteousness which man cannot achieve for himself is offered to him by God in Jesus Christ and can be received by faith, by the trusting acceptance of the word of promise in Jesus Christ.

Objections!

Two powerful objections have consistently been made against this teaching. The first is that it involves God in the unethical business of treating man as righteous when in fact he is not. Unless some arrangement can be made so that man actually achieves some measure of righteousness, he cannot enter into a real and living relationship with God – so the argument goes. But Paul declares that there is no contradiction between God's love and his holiness. God is holy, yes; but because he loves us he has made a way by which righteousness can be restored to his creation. To be united through faith with the Christ who is the revelation of God *is* righteousness. Man can never earn nor deserve God's approval. It can only come as a gift. Trust in God is the proper relationship to God, and this relationship is righteousness.

The second objection is that justification by faith destroys ethics and morality. 'What shall we say, then? Shall we go on sinning, so that grace may increase?' If man is accounted righteous apart from ethical accomplishment and moral endeavour, he will have no concern for others – so the argument goes. However, this ignores both the cross and the judgment. In the cross God has unmistakably demonstrated his hatred and condemnation of sin. In the judgment faith is assessed by its fruits. Indifference to sin and evil or neglect of the responsibilities of the life in Christ cannot be defended. Ethical indifference as a lifestyle does *not* follow from justification by faith, but is the substitution of an impersonal moral or legal relationship for the true, vibrant, warm personal relationship to God which is offered to us in the gospel.

The full scope of redemption

The apostle Paul's emphasis on justification by faith alone occurs throughout his writings – but nowhere more powerfully than in his letter to the Colossians. Other teachers had followed him in Colossae and taught that what God had done in Jesus was not sufficient and the worshipper must, in addition to his faith and trust in the work of Christ, worship certain 'spiritual rulers and authorities' and submit to special rites, such as circumcision, and observe obscure rules about food and other matters. In other words forgiveness and freedom were dependent not only on what God had done in Christ, but also on what we were prepared to do and were able to do. So Paul confidently and triumphantly declares: 'You were at one time spiritually dead [requiring resurrection and reformation!] because of your sins and because you were Gentiles without the Law. But God has now brought you to life with Christ. God forgave us all our sins; he cancelled the unfavourable record of our debts with its binding rules and did away with it completely by nailing it to the cross' (Colossians 2:13 and 14). So God's method of forgiveness is to *cancel* our 'unfavourable record' of debts. The Greek word translated 'cancelled' is *exaleiphō* and it occurs only five times in the New Testament. One of its uses is of the greatest significance in this whole area of forgiveness. In classical Greek the word begins by meaning 'to wash over'. It is used, for instance, of 'whitewashing' the wall of a house. It is used of warriors 'painting' their bodies with war paint. It is used of 'anointing' with oil. The word developed the meaning of 'to wipe out or obliterate'. It is so used of 'wiping out' a memory of an experience from one's remembrance or one's mind; of 'cancelling' a vote or 'annulling' a law; of 'cancelling' a charge or a debt or of 'striking a man's name off a roll' or list; of 'wiping a family completely out of existence'. Always it has this meaning of wiping something out or obliterating something as you would chalk writing on a slate with a sponge.

In the New Testament it is not always used literally. In Revelation 7:17 and 21:4 it is used of 'wiping away' the tears from every eye. In Revelation 3:5 it is used for 'wiping out' a man's name from a roll. In Acts 3:19 it is used for wiping out sin: 'Repent, then, and turn to God, so that he will forgive your sins' (literally: 'that your sins be wiped away' or as the Authorised Version puts it 'that your sins may be blotted out').

It is in this context that the word and concept is used in Colossians 2:14. The 'unfavourable record' that Paul speaks of there is a *cheirographos* – a document which acknowledges a debt that had to be paid. It was this debt that Jesus wiped out for us. In New Testament times documents were written on papyrus. The ink was made of soot, mixed with gum and diluted with water. The characteristic of this ink was that it had no acid in it and therefore did not bite into the paper. It lasts a very long time and retains its colour but if, soon after it was written, a wet sponge was passed over the surface of the papyrus, the writing could be sponged off as completely as writing might be sponged from a slate.

However, the interesting thing is that a commoner word for cancelling a certificate of debt was *chiazō*. *Chiazō* means to write the Greek letter chi, which is the same shape as a capital X, right across the document. So, after a trial in Egypt, the governor might give orders that a bond should be cancelled (*chiazō*), that is, 'crossed out'. But Paul does not say that Jesus 'crossed out' (*chiazō*) the record of our debt; he says that he 'wiped it out' (*exaleiphō*). If you 'cross a thing out', beneath the cross the record still remains visible for anyone to read. But if you 'wipe it out' the record is gone, obliterated for ever. There is many a man who can forgive, but the memory of the wrong lingers in the subconscious if not always in the conscious mind. But God's forgiveness is that supreme forgiveness which not only forgives but also forgets. Our wrong-doing is not only out of sight, it is out of mind.

Our calling to forgive
Our forgiveness of others is to be as God has forgiven us. It is the wonder of the reality of our own forgiveness and total acceptance by God that is the powerful motive and driving force for us, when we are hurt and humiliated and disadvantaged, still to be willing to take the initiative and forgive. Our forgiveness of others may well be costly and painful just as it cost God to forgive us. Our forgiveness is the result of the sheer undeserved generosity of the heart of God. Emil Brunner puts it so clearly in his book *The Mediator*:

In the Cross of Christ God says to man, 'That is where you ought to be. Jesus my Son hangs there in your stead. His tragedy is the tragedy of your life. You are the rebel who should be hanged on the gallows. But lo, I suffered instead of you, and because of you, because I love you in spite of what you are. My love for you is so great that I meet you

there, there on the Cross. I cannot meet you anywhere else. You must meet me there by identifying
yourself with the One on the Cross. It is by this
identification that I, God, can meet you in Him,
saying to you as I say to Him, My beloved Son.'

Most of us struggle with forgiving others completely
because we have not fully recognised how much we have
been forgiven by God and the cost and pain involved in
making that possible for us.

I remember the first time I visited York. I was immediately struck by the atmosphere of history. It did not
require too much imagination to see men and women of
a different era in vastly different dress walk the narrow
streets. The Minster dominated the city – it seemed to
have been there forever, watching, hoping, waiting.
Inside it was awesome – its size, its height, its architecture,
its windows, its atmosphere. However, it was in a much
smaller church building that I discovered a commemorative tablet about a certain Canon Faussett. I had never
heard of him, and in any case most churches seem to have
their fair share of commemorative tablets and give the
impression that they honour the past by living in it rather
than learning from it. This particular church dignitary had
one event in his life which is little known – but then
who does know anything about Canon Faussett? Like a
number of clergy of his day he owned land in Ireland.
Land there was cheap to buy and provided an investment
of sorts in those days – especially for those who had a bit
of money, but were not particularly rich. During one of
the potato famines some of the families who lived on
his estate found themselves completely destitute and so
unable to pay their rent to him, the landlord. In their
impossible situation they wrote to Canon Faussett begging
him to let them off in view of their unforeseen circumstances. Were they not entitled to believe that a leader
in the church would respond mercifully to them? To their
dismay the landlord replied that he could never accede

to their request. It would set a bad precedent, it was wrong, and he couldn't possibly make an exception in spite of his understanding of their desperate situation. He insisted that they must pay their bills to the last penny. However, in his letter of reply to their request in which he refused to excuse their payment of the rent he enclosed a slip of paper. It was a cheque, for more than sufficient to cover all that they owed him.

In a very limited and vastly imperfect way that is a tiny picture of what God accomplished through Jesus' death on the cross for us, in order that two things might be secured – our forgiveness and his justice and righteousness.

Forgiveness is infinitely more than 'shaking hands and going home'. It is concluding that forgiveness is not to be withheld; that forgiveness is a decision which is consciously and honourably taken; that never, as children of God, are we more like our Father than when we forgive; and that as we choose to forgive so God the Holy Spirit comes alongside us to enable us to make it real. It is only at the cross that the full dimension of forgiveness can be glimpsed. Voltaire, the French philosopher, once said, 'Of course God forgives sin; that's his business.' There is no 'of course' anywhere in the New Testament. The powerful and wonderful revelation of the Christian gospel is that God can forgive sin, but only through the cross of his Son, Jesus Christ.

It is only as we see this that wonderingly and adoringly can we receive forgiveness and honestly and generously can we give it. It is to this demanding reality that we are called – to forgive as those who have been so completely and perfectly forgiven.

2
With his head under his arm!

I had left the National Exhibition Centre in Birmingham, where I had shared in an international conference, and travelled north through the lovely countryside of Cumbria, the borders and the Grampian region to the Moray Firth. I was to share there in another conference. The initial launching of the Scottish conference was quite demanding and after a few days I was glad to have a break. The programme allowed for this one afternoon and I drove about a mile from the hotel where I was staying and parked the car where I could look across the firth to the hills of Cromarty and Fortrose and beyond to Invergordon. I read and slept without getting out of the car until I decided it was time to get back to the hotel to get the rest of the day's programme organised. I drove the mile back and parked a little carelessly outside the hotel. When I tried to start the car to 'straighten up' a bit, it wouldn't start. I'm no car expert, but I do know how to open the bonnet and look underneath. I checked the leads and connections I could see and all seemed in order until I noticed a small cylinder which appeared to have come off its mounting. Oil was flowing freely out of it all over the engine and on to the ground. Even I knew this must be the cause of the problem. Inside the hotel was Raymond – another member of the conference team. He was expert on cars! He came and looked with a swift eye at what I had described, and expressed great surprise. 'I cannot understand how you have driven from London to Birmingham and then to the north of Scotland with your distributor loose,' he said. 'The distributor is the brain of the engine and gives instructions to the other parts how to function. I cannot believe what I am seeing. It is rather like you telling me that you just saw a man walking down the High Street with his head under his arm! It really is impossible for a car to function when the distributor is improperly connected!'

I was unable then, as I am unable now, to clear the matter up for Raymond. He found some bolts in another part of the engine and secured the distributor so that I was able to drive to a garage and have the repair done and consequently drive home without incident. Forgiveness is anything but mechanical, but it is a bit like that all-important distributor in that it is vital. Neither corporately nor individually is it possible to function properly when forgiveness is absent. To expect to live whole lives without forgiveness is as unrealistic as to claim that you just saw a man walking down the High Street with his head under his arm. That is silly because it is impossible. Living in right relationships with one another through the expression and experience of forgiveness is as necessary to a living faith as the head is to the living human body.

Release from darkness

Why is forgiveness so important? First of all because it is part of the process which releases us from the powers of darkness. To be involved in kingdom life, and so to move in the power of the Holy Spirit, is to get immediately into confrontation with the powers of darkness. This is neither to be feared nor to be denied, but is to be accepted as one of the facts experienced by the obedient, submissive servant of the living God. After Jesus' baptism in the Jordan by John, and his anointing by the Spirit (Luke 3:21,22), he was immediately led into confrontation with the devil (Luke 4:1–13). Jesus' real battle was neither with the politics of the occupying Roman power nor with the entrenched, ritualistic, legalistic tradition of the Jewish religion – although both of these did create many difficulties for him – it was with the powers of darkness. This dangerous opposition had to be recognised by Jesus right at the beginning; and that particular battle had to be fought and won before real ministry could begin. But in the evangelical church in which I grew up, this area was either totally ignored or successfully glossed over. I cannot recall any mention being made of this, or any instruction being given as I prepared and trained for the ordained ministry. I had been ordained and gone through two pastorates before I became aware of areas in pastoral caring in which the deepest care was ineffective, and of problems which defiantly persisted in spite of my ministering regularly and faithfully as pastor. And this in some of the loveliest people I have known! Something was missing; a dimension was absent; a key had been lost somewhere.

It was only in the late 'sixties that I became aware of the tremendous rise in spiritism and satanic activity in this country. There were insidious expressions of satanic activity that made inroads into the lives of ordinary men and women – ouija boards were common, horoscopes had become increasingly popular, séances had proliferated, black magic was practised, and satanic worship was no longer the pursuit of the fringe few. The debunking of God within our society; the increasing depersonalisation which was taking place in all kinds of spheres of life; the disenchantment that many were experiencing with science and technology as the answer to human woes and frustrations; the disillusionment with the church that had occurred post World War I and World War II – all created a spiritual vacuum that demanded to be filled. Man is by his very nature religious – and if this questing, hungry aspect of our nature is not satisfied by truth and light it will quickly gravitate towards, and attempt to be satisfied with, error and darkness.

As I began to develop in the ministry of the Holy Spirit, determined to be satisfied with nothing less than honesty and reality, or else depart from the ministry altogether, I discovered that I was becoming almost overwhelmed in pastoral work by Christian casualties. Maybe my situation was accentuated by the fact that we, as a church, are relatively close to the British headquarters of two large and fine interdenominational and international missionary societies plus an academically responsible and Bible-based Bible college. Some people from these organisations (people who loved the Lord and were prepared to lay their lives on the line to serve him) – fine Christians – were deeply depressed, or apparently unrescuably defeated, or oppressed irrationally and devastatingly by some dark powers, or suddenly filled with numbing doubts or bitter resentment and aware that they were in need of deliverance. Missionary leaders shared their concerns with me that a significant percentage of those trained, commissioned and sent out to serve the Lord overseas were invalided out through breakdowns of one kind or another or persistent illnesses that were difficult to diagnose. It was becoming clearer to them, and to me, that there was a whole dimension of spiritual warfare to which, as evangelical Christians, we paid scant regard.

So it was that in the very early 'seventies my wife, Anne, and I became involved in what is referred to as deliverance ministry. Only a few years previously I would have thought this bizarre, suspect, and hardly fitting in the context of respectable pastoring. It became so demanding on time and energy that within a year or two we had to recognise that this much-needed ministry was becoming so absorbing that the responsibilities which I had been called to carry in the local church were being neglected. Those were days of lonely decisions, since a plural leadership was present but not yet functioning effectively in our church. There were certain lessons we learnt.

We discovered, for example, that the first base for deliverance from any intrusive, invading power of darkness that had come to make its presence real in a godly life was *humility*. I need deliverance. That may be difficult to accept, but I have concluded that we can either have our dignity or our deliverance – and often it is not possible to have both! The next base in deliverance is a painful but necessary *honesty*.

The third base is *confession*. I have never been sure of the dynamics of this, but I do know that something happens when I make a clear confession – whether it is to the fact that Jesus Christ is Lord or to the fact that there is something wrong in my life that I recognise and which needs dealing with.

The fourth base is *renunciation*. Deliverance involves an act of the will. God will only deliver us from our enemies, not our friends. As long as we desire and court and caress an area of our lives which is wrong then it will remain firmly entrenched there. The decision to be free must result in a willing discipline so to organise and reorientate my life that I give clear evidence that I want to be free.

The fifth base, however, is crucial to the whole exercise. It is the *forgiveness of all others*. We discover that two of the devil's favourite loopholes by which entry is gained into an unsuspecting, godly life are interest in the occult (and often we are blissfully unaware of how significant that interest is) and unforgiveness. How often I had attached a condition to my forgiveness: if the other person saw the error of his ways, was properly sorry, and admitted his guilt – then, as a Christian, I had an obligation to forgive him. But I had to come to the place where I clearly realised that these were *my* fixed set of conditions, not Christ's. The scope and inflexibility of Jesus' teaching on forgiveness is straightforward and staggering. 'And when you stand and pray,' he said, 'forgive anything you may have against anyone, so that your Father in heaven will forgive the wrongs you have done' (Mark 11:25). I may protest and struggle with the unfairness of forgiveness, the justification of why I should withhold my forgiveness, and the possible abuse of my forgiveness – and yet forgive I must. Forgiveness means: 'the other person may be as wrong as wrong can be, but I'll not be the judge.' As we have already affirmed, forgiveness is simply the decision of our will to release a particular person followed by verbalising that to God. In practical terms we can use a formula like, 'Lord, I release . . . from my judgment. Forgive me that I may have bound him and hampered your work in him and through him by judging him. Now I willingly and consciously step out of the way so that you and the resources of heaven can go into action for. . . .' There is nothing difficult about using that formula. It is much more difficult to use it honestly and with uncluttered sincerity. The difficulty must be faced, however. The faith to believe that such a non-emotional release will result in changes in the other person's life is another matter altogether. However, we must attend to our part and trust God to attend to his.

There are many examples of the effectiveness of such a course, but the Biblical example that will come to mind most readily is that of Stephen, the first Christian martyr (Acts 7). As his flesh was torn and his bones broken by stones hurled, not so much in anger as in calculated judgment, Saul of Tarsus stood dispassionately by. 'Lord!' Stephen shouted, 'Do not remember this sin against them!' In other words, 'I forgive them!' Stephen's release of Saul and the others made it possible for God to go into powerful action. Powerful indeed – stopped in his tracks, prostrated, blinded, overwhelmed on the Damascus road, Saul of Tarsus became Paul the Apostle – missionary of the gospel par excellence, contender for the faith, apostle to the Gentiles and spiritual father to all of us in the western world (Acts 9).

The final stage of release is when I *call on the name of Jesus*. He is the only one who can deliver – there is no hope of real and lasting freedom anywhere else. He delivers by the power of his Holy Spirit. Jesus himself affirmed the Spirit's power to set men free when he was confronted by controversy over his own ministry. 'No,' he said, 'it is not Beelzebul, but God's Spirit, who gives me the power to drive out demons, which proves that the Kingdom of God has already come upon you' (Matthew 12:28).

Free to serve

Not only does forgiveness have a vital part to play in the process of releasing us from captivity to the powers of darkness, but secondly forgiveness will free us to serve God. Christian service is not the pursuit of the chosen few, but the obligation of everyone who has been redeemed by Jesus Christ. Someone once said that any gospel which cannot save us out of selfishness into service will never save us out of hell into heaven. 'God has made us as we are,' writes the apostle Paul, 'and in our union with Christ Jesus he has created us for a life of good deeds, which he has already prepared for us to do' (Ephesians 2:10). Nothing will mar and impair our service more readily than a heart that remains impervious to the forgiving love of God.

No matter how gifted, able, effective and significant the servant of the Lord, his ministry will be spoiled by a stubborn resentment and a resistant animosity which is not released in forgiveness. It is said that when Leonardo da Vinci was painting his great masterpiece, the Last Supper, he decided to paint Judas with the features of a man who had hurt and maligned him in the past. Ugliness and evil were etched on these features out of the bitterness of Leonardo's own heart. All had gone well until that point. Having completed Judas' features with the malignant memories of past hurts, however, Leonardo's genius seemed to dry up. No matter how hard he tried he could not continue what he had begun. Puzzled and frustrated, it was only in a moment of revelation that Leonardo became aware of the reason. When he was prepared to obliterate his former friend's features his genius began to flow again.

The cost of unforgiveness is too high – an unfulfilled and fruitless life – and none of us can afford to pay that kind of price. Life is too short, the task is too great, the opportunities are too few to be bedevilled by anything which would spoil the purpose for which we were created and redeemed.

Forgiveness heals

Forgiveness is important, thirdly, because it can release *physical healing*. People are body-soul-spirit beings. No one would doubt that physical tiredness will dull the emotions, blunt the will, cause weariness to the mind and heaviness in the spirit. Soaring emotions will revitalise the body, quicken the mind, activate the will and lift the spirit. In other words each part of our being has a profound effect on every other part, for good or ill.

In a remarkable happening in Capernaum (Mark 2:1–12) we read of a strangely passive, silent man who is paralysed. He never does anything nor does he ask any questions until after he has been healed. Maybe his condition had frustrated him for such a long time that his permanent outlook was now despair and pessimism. It seems that this man's life was transformed through the faith of his friends. How much all of us owe to those who love us and care for us we will never be able to assess. There is no record of co-operation, encouragement, or gratitude from this man to anyone. Surprising as all of this is, the most surprising feature of the story is that Jesus implies in his treatment of him that his problem is not really sickness but sin. It is not his body that has the greatest need, but his spirit. In our culture we would say it is not a doctor he needs, but a clergyman – although all the presenting symptoms are to the contrary.

How little we really know about the real nature of our need! In these days when diet has become so important in our society we need to affirm again – at least in general terms – that it is not what we eat that causes most difficulty for us, but what eats us. So often it is not food which is our problem, but our need of forgiveness. Trenchantly, Thomas Aquinas affirms that grace flows from the soul to the body. And in the incident Mark records, Jesus clearly indicates that paralysis is not the first issue – pardon is. It is not so much freedom in his body that he ultimately needs as forgiveness in his spirit.

Undoubtedly sin and sickness are connected, although my sickness is not always the result of my sin. Jesus made this clear in his dealing with the blind man in the Gospel of John (9:3). However, while Jesus was concerned to meet the physical, material, tangible needs of men and women – and the gospels record that he spent two-thirds of his ministry doing this – nevertheless he was much more concerned to make people whole. He was aware that then, as now, men and women have a pre-occupation – maybe even an obsession – with the physical, whereas he was also deeply concerned about the spiritual. We, so often, are concerned with health, whilst he is also concerned with holiness. We view life so much in terms of this world and our earthly home, while he gives perspective to this world by reminding us constantly of the next world and our eternal home. After all, this is the land of the dying and we are yet to inhabit the land of the living.

It is in this context that forgiveness needs to find its real place – and that is often connected with our physical well-being.

Forgiveness releases prayer

Forgiveness has a significant effect in our confidence in

praying. Jesus affirms that there is a close connection between faith and forgiveness, and between the miraculous and the moral in prayer.

> For this reason I tell you: When you pray and ask for something, believe that you have received it, and you will be given whatever you ask for. And when you stand and pray, forgive anything you may have against anyone, so that your Father in heaven will forgive the wrongs you have done (Mark 11:24,25).

This is a powerful and practical statement on prayer by the one who alone is the master when it comes to praying. Through the years, in my own fumbling and human way, I have come to discover that there are five things which cause a hindrance in praying.

Doubt is one of the hindrances to prayer. In his very practical little letter to second generation Christians James writes:

> But when you pray, you must believe and not doubt at all. Whoever doubts is like a wave in the sea that is driven and blown about by the wind. A person like that, unable to make up his mind and undecided in all he does, must not think that he will receive anything from the Lord (James 1:6–8).

A second hindrance is *praying out of God's will*. That wise old campaigner, chosen by Jesus in his young manhood, but now possibly one hundred years old, John, writes so helpfully:

> We have courage in God's presence, because we are sure that he hears us if we ask him for anything that is according to his will. He hears us whenever we ask him; and since we know that this is true, we know also that he gives us what we ask from him (1 John 5:14).

A third hindrance to answered prayer is the *opposition of Satan*. Many things are attractive in Christian praying:

Christian prayer is *to* the Father – God is listening and attentive; *through* the Son – Jesus is involved in heaven before his Father when we pray; *by* the Spirit – the Holy Spirit is enabling us as we struggle with the weakness and limitation of our humanity on earth; *with* the saints – there is a great company of believers who join with us so often in the things which concern and burden us; and *against* the devil.

> We are not fighting against human beings but against the wicked spiritual forces in the heavenly world, the rulers, authorities, and cosmic powers of this dark age (Ephesians 6:12).

Another hindrance to answered prayer is *sin and guilt* in our lives, which we either justify or ignore. The heartcry of the psalmist needs to be heeded today when he says:

> If I had ignored my sins,
>   the Lord would not have listened to me.
> But God has indeed heard me;
>   he has listened to my prayer (Psalm 66:18).

The word translated here 'ignored' really means 'to caress', 'to fondle'. It means a willing acceptance of and delight in what I know God disallows. There is a surfeit of desire for riches and cleverness and power in our society (and even in our churches), but an absence of godliness and desire for righteousness. God does not overlook this or take it lightly.

Finally, unanswered prayer is hindered by an *unforgiving and resentful spirit*. We can have no confidence in our praying, and expect no response to our praying, as long as we ignore the mandatory direction to forgive 'anything' and 'everyone' (Mark 11:25).

Over the years I have found it necessary to pray constantly for those who have spoken against me, hurt me, made life difficult for me, criticised me, and set me in a bad light before others. I have found it helpful to my own hurt thinking to consider that they may not actually have said or done what I have been told that they said and did (ie if the hurt, criticism or action was in my absence and has been reported to me). Secondly, I need to consider carefully that what they have said or done may have been right. Maybe the areas where I have been attacked and put under threat need to be looked at with a view to making some changes. Thirdly, it is possible that those who have injured me may already be sorry for what they have said and done. After all, my own life is marked by things which make me far from proud, and I have found it so difficult to know how and when to say I am sorry. I am also aware that even if none of these three factors is relevant, it is never a mistake to pray for them – and to continue praying until there is nothing but love present in my heart for them. It is difficult to the point of impossibility really to pray for someone and still bear a grudge and have resentment in your heart. Most of us have friends on our prayer list (and there is nothing wrong with that!), but the Bible says that the sick, those in positions of authority within society and our *enemies* should be on our prayer list. Perhaps this is prayer-list examination time!! The best way to remove our enemies is to make them our friends – and praying for them will go a long way to achieving this.

Forgiveness is Christlike

Forgiveness is important because to forgive is to express the character of God. God's whole attitude is forgiving love. He does not turn a blind eye to wrong and pretend that it does not matter. There is no weak sentimentality in the character of God. To forgive us and put us back into fellowship is costly and painful. It cost God his own Son, and Jesus went through the agony of being separated from his Father and undergoing the humiliation of death on a cross. God does not wait for people to come humbly and contritely back asking for forgiveness – long ago he took the initiative.

If I looked through the spy-hole of my front door one night and saw a man standing there who was six feet five in height, with wide shoulders, thick neck, a barrel-chest, and huge fists at the end of very ample arms I would be glad of the spy-hole, the light in the porch that revealed the reality of the caller, and the thickness of my front door with its secure lock and double-sure chain. However, I would want to know two more things about my visitor standing there. First of all I would want to know what kind of man he was – violent or peaceful, placid or short-tempered, reasonable or irrational. Secondly, I would want to know why he had come to me – as a friend or with a grievance, to express kindness or settle a score. It is only if I was sure of both these things that I would be prepared to undo the chain and unlock the door. His attitudes and intentions are much more important to me than his attributes.

Few would doubt God's power. Every tiny atom in the universe which God has made is packed with enormous power. Enormous power is needed to hurl a space rocket out of earth's gravitational pull: can we begin to visualise the sort of power needed to get the earth itself into orbit, or pack the sun with the energy that fills our solar system? It is that power which is at God's disposal – inconceivable power.

However, the issue that really concerns me is not so much God's attributes – his greatness, power, eternity, creativity and so on – as his attitudes and intentions. How does God feel? What is he like? What motivates his actions? God has clearly declared his intention – he does not desire the destruction or condemnation of any, but he comes in Christ to redeem us. God has also demonstrated his love – through his Son whom he sent into our world.

In Shakespeare's play *Measure for Measure* the author deals with the dilemma of imperfect people trying to apply the laws of perfect morality. In the story-line an apparently upright judge distorts justice under the sudden temptation to lust. He declines to offer mercy to a young man guilty of the very sin he himself is contemplating. The play, with typical skill, probes all the deep questions that this raises. If Shakespeare could be said to have reached any conclusion it is probably summed up in a few words just before the final curtain:

They say, best men are moulded out of faults;
And, for the most, become much more the better
For being a little bad.

In other words, in an imperfect world we must learn to live with imperfection, tempering justice with mercy and being tolerant of the faults of others, knowing that we often have the same faults ourselves.

God moves in another dimension altogether. He himself has taken the punishment and condemnation of righteous judgment upon himself – so enabling us to enter into freedom from punishment and condemnation because he has borne it on our behalf. The Bible affirms that Jesus, who was sinless, became sin on our behalf, enabling a pure and holy God to remain righteous and yet offer us forgiveness and hope.

This lies at the heart of our gospel. Never do we more clearly demonstrate the nature of God himself than when we forgive those who have wronged us. If we would know the deepest reality of fellowship with God we must learn to forgive others as he has forgiven us. Forgiveness lies at the heart of his character and to touch his heart we too need to forgive.

For all these reasons, then, forgiveness is so important and needs to be understood and pursued with all the eagerness we can engender. And the search is not fruitless because of the grace that God so lavishly pours out upon us.

3
Follow the instructions!

I was staying at a home where there were four children. The eldest was thoughtful, sensitive, mature for his years. Maybe even at this early stage realising that he was the eldest of the family. One of his hobbies was paper-folding – origami.

A number of 'creations' emerged during my stay with his family. I realised that I had always wanted to be good at paper-folding. Maybe it was an idle ambition – but I was fascinated. This boy let me into his secret – a book of straightforward diagrams with very simple, clear instructions. It worked for him, so why not for me? I started at the third from the beginning – after all, I was an adult and it was a bit humiliating to start at the very beginning. He was well on towards the end of the book anyway. But it didn't work for me! With careful patience he encouraged me to try again. 'All you need to do is to follow the instructions carefully', he said, 'and you'll see it works.' I did, but it didn't – well, not quite. 'You need to keep trying', he said, 'and you'll see that it works.'

I have been back home for several weeks now and I haven't even considered a piece of paper with a view to folding it and making something that would satisfy my young friend. I suppose he would dismiss me as a failed origami expert. Many things are like that – we say that we want something, but we never have it because we give up too quickly. Forgiveness requires patience and persistence in following the steps, and seeing that it works. But we find that it doesn't work as simply as we thought it would, or the way the book said it should – and we settle for failure. Like everything else, forgiveness is a learned process, but it can be a hard lesson to learn.

It's tough!

The classic set of circumstances is that someone hurt you – maybe this morning, or yesterday, or a long time ago, and you cannot get it out of your mind. On reflection – and the details are clear and in very sharp focus in your mind – you did not deserve what was said or done to you. It was unfair, maybe even quite untrue. It is there now like a thorn in the point of your finger – lodged deeply in your memory with the tone of voice, the expression on the face, the avoiding eyes, the clear body language, the other people involved who didn't need to hear or see what was done, or even the cold print of a letter – and it hurts. No matter what you do it hurts. No matter how determined you are to get on with the rest of your life and put it out of your mind, it hurts.

It does not help a great deal to know that you are not alone. All of us muddle our way through a world where well-meaning people hurt each other. A long-standing friend with whom we have shared so deeply through the years betrays us. A parent abuses us, not only in childhood, but in adult life. A son or daughter disregards us and speaks or acts in a disparaging and insensitive way. A husband or wife leaves us – alone, humiliated, rejected. These situations are all around me as I ride on the tube at rush-hour, as I sit in the nose-to-tail traffic jam on the motorway, as I go to the theatre or the football match, as I pay attention to my list and fill my trolley in the supermarket, as I rise to sing the next hymn in church. But it doesn't help me. The situation and the circumstances are peculiar to me, and it hurts.

Hannah Arendt, the philosopher, discovered as she explored human behaviour, response and reaction that the only power which can stop the stream of painful memories is 'the faculty of forgiving'. One December day in 1983 Pope John Paul II walked into the prison cell where Mehmet Ali Agca had been incarcerated. There the two men met. Agca had fired a bullet at the pope's heart. Whatever his motive, his intention was to destroy the pope. In a quiet moment alone with his would-be assassin, the pope forgave him.

A much less publicised incident occurred when Barnardo, a medical student in east London, was involved in a riot in a public house. He had gone in to sell Bibles, but many inside the public house were already drunk beyond reason and attacked him with fury. Barnado was flung to the ground and a table was placed upside down on his prostrate body, and the pub clientele danced on it. When he was removed, unconscious, to his lodgings he was bruised from head to foot and had two broken ribs. It was six weeks before he could move about again. Not unnaturally, the police got involved, and Barnardo was pressed to prosecute the ringleaders. He refused. 'I have begun with the gospel,' he said, 'and I am determined not to end with the Law.'

For most of us, however, it is not easy to forgive. We may well assume that the pope and a man of the calibre of Dr Barnardo (as he came to be known and respected) are outstanding human beings. We may conclude that things are different for ordinary people like ourselves. We need to realise that forgiveness is never easy for anyone. To forgive seems unnatural. There is something within us, our sense of fairness, which tells us that people should pay for the wrong they do. Hate – our natural response to deep and unfair wounds – comes more easily. A woman hopes earnestly that her former husband will be miserable and desperately unhappy with his new wife. A man hopes that the friend who sold him short and blatantly betrayed him will find himself redundant and struggling to make ends meet and maintain his standard of living. Passive or aggressive, hate is a malignancy that festers and grows, stifling joy and often threatening our health. Although we recognise that hate always hurts the hater more than the hated, we persist in finding a macabre satisfaction in it, and resist releasing the hated. It is a peculiarly self-destructive attitude which grips and over-rides our reason. Whatever forgiveness might do for the one needing to be forgiven, we need to forgive for our own sake. This is recognised by many, but so persistently ignored. Forgiving, difficult as it is, can bring a miraculous kind of healing not only to the forgiven, but also to the forgiver.

The challenge that confronts us is – how can this be done? How can you let go of a grievance, a hurting memory, a destructive resentment? What shall we do?

Confront reality

First of all we need to confront the reality of our resentment, hatred, animosity and hurt towards the other person. None of us wants to admit these things. Playing down how we feel; claiming we do not really feel that way; pretending that things are different from what they really are; putting a brave face on it; maintaining a polite facade – all are part of the mechanism which enables us to ward off reality. But the fiery denial rages corrosively beneath the surface like some subterranean storm, polluting all our relationships. Admitting that we are hurt, sore, resentful, critical and condemning compels us to make a decision about the soul surgery we call forgiving. Somehow or other we must face up to the situation that we have been wronged and we need to do something about it. Pretending or protesting otherwise will not do a thing for us – or for 'them'.

I can remember sitting at my desk – alone in my home

– in my little upstairs study with its high window looking over Dumbarton. I had been ordained a few months previously and these were demanding, exhilarating days. The task of preaching at least three times every week to the same congregation was proving to be a daunting assignment. I was regulating my week as best I knew how so that I could reasonably cope. On this particular morning in early spring I was beginning to prepare early in the week for the coming weekend. Nothing came. I could not make a beginning! I tried to pray. I read my Bible. I looked at one or two books. I scanned some magazine articles. Nothing! Had I dried up so quickly? Nobody had ever told me it would be easy to be a minister, but neither had I been told it would be this difficult. What should I do? Where could I go? Who could I turn to? I could think of nothing; nobody. Here I was, trapped in my little study with its blue carpet, its somewhat outsize desk for the size of the room, its few books, its high window. Not even a cup of coffee and a chocolate Vienna biscuit helped. Alone, uncomfortable, anxious, near to panic – I had no other direction in which to move. I prayed.

God answered. He, astonishingly, put it into my heart that I was resentful towards my father. He had married my stepmother too soon (I thought!) after my mother's tragic death and had expected me to receive her not only as his wife, but as my mother. I couldn't! I did not want to! I was offended and hurt by it all. My own bereavement was not yet complete. I felt I needed to become independent and stand on my own two feet, but I didn't know how to. I was angry at being forced into a position which left me confused. The animosity between my mother's family and my father over his new marriage only increased my own unhappiness and distress. Where did my loyalty lie? I could not please everybody, and I was in great danger of pleasing nobody.

I had only just gone up to university and I was finding that difficult enough – travelling every day, looking after myself in my own family home now vacated by my brother (because he had married) and largely deserted by my father because, apart from working, he spent most of his time with the lady he was intending to marry. It was not that anything was particularly wrong; but I felt that not everything was right. Many times I comforted myself with self-pity. I hated the resentment that welled up in my heart. The fine lady who was to become my stepmother seemed kind and was obviously trying to understand me. She couldn't – nor did I want her to. My silence and withdrawn behaviour towards all family matters must have been hurtful and unbelievably difficult to handle.

That morning in my study in Dumbarton it all came flooding back. It seemed an unusual response from God (if that was its source!) to my heart-cry for help. I have no idea how long my interview with God went on, but he laid insistently on my heart, 'You need to forgive your father. Go and put things right with him.' I protested that I could not recall ever saying anything that was rude or hurtful or impertinent to him during the period that I was now recalling so vividly. 'You said nothing, but your attitude was cold and distant and you conveyed disapproval and condemnation,' God seemed to counter. I could not deny that.

This dialogue was not audible – I did not hear God speak to me through my physical ears – and yet it was painfully real. That morning I poured out my confession to the Lord and, alone in my study, expressed my forgiveness of my father. I determined that I should go and see him that evening and put things right between us. My preparation for the Sunday services began to flow. That night I called on my father and apologised for my behaviour. To my great discomfort he seemed blissfully unaware of what I was talking about. I will never know what was really in his heart, but one thing I do know is that he was one of my greatest encouragers through all my years of ministry until the day when he went to be with the Lord. My stepmother became my friend and our relationship deepened until the day when she too went to be with the Lord.

In admitting the reality of my resentment towards my godly father I made a decision about forgiveness. Such an admission is never easy, because we know so often that we should not feel that way or be like that. But there is no other way to go if we are going to walk in freedom with God. This is the first major step: *confront reality*.

See clearly
The next step in learning to forgive is to *separate the wrong-doer from the wrong*. It is possible to be angry at the deed without continuing to be angry with the doer. In the Old Testament the graphic, unusual drama of the atonement is described in detail. It tells how God commanded that the high priest confess the sins of the people over a goat, chosen for the purpose, and that the goat should, symbolically, bear those sins away to a 'solitary land'. This vivid visual aid (from which we get the term 'scapegoat') showed that God had separated the wrong-doer from the wrong, so that he could continue to bless the people.

Forgiving is finding a new attitude, a new vision, a new response to the person who has wronged you. It is the demand of our wills to see the person who is behind the actions. It is possible to do this and discover a new insight about the person who has wronged us. As we come to see the deeper truth about people – that they are needy, apprehensive, fallible, insecure human beings – our feelings change.

As we determine to separate the wrong-doer from the wrong, surely the Holy Spirit joins us to strengthen and enable us to handle the natural upsurge in our being of desire for revenge and retaliation and to declare, as Jesus did on the cross: 'They do not know what they are doing.'

Let go!
The third step in learning to forgive is to *let go of the past*. Forgetting the past is often not possible for us, but letting go the painful memories of the snub, the piece

of sarcasm, the contemptuous word, the unfairness, the injustice, the misrepresentation, the incident that led to life being so much more difficult than it need have been, *is* possible. Others may well have long forgotten, but we cannot. What we can do is determine to take steps to let the past go. There is an elemental passion in human nature for revenge. Christ can and does, however, take from our hearts the slow, deep fire of resentment, and give us love instead of hate. Hard as it is, it is possible. Strenuous though the spiritual discipline may be, it is healthy. Foolish as it may seem to the wise ones of this world, it is wonderfully effective. Granted our willingness and co-operation, he can enable us to release the past.

Keep at it!

Fourthly, we need to be powerfully persuaded never to give up at forgiveness but to *keep working at it*. As a boy, C S Lewis, the agnostic who was to become one of the most popular Christian apologists of this century, was badly hurt by a bully of a school teacher. For most of his life Lewis could not forgive this teacher, and being a failure at forgiving troubled him. But not long before he died, Lewis wrote to a friend: 'Only a few weeks ago I suddenly realised that I had at last forgiven the school teacher who so darkened my childhood. I'd been trying to do it for years and each time I thought I'd done it, I found it had to be attempted again. But this time, I feel sure it is the real thing.'

We are prone to give up too quickly and to give in too easily. So many things have only been accomplished by men and women who have persevered when others might have given up. In the middle of the nineteenth century there was a man called Samuel Plimsoll. He was a friend of sailors. In those days greedy and self-seeking ship-owners sent sailors out in what came to be known as 'coffin-ships'. In the first instance these ships were unseaworthy, but they were loaded in such a way as to make them highly dangerous. They were sent to sea so heavily insured that even if they were lost the owners would not lose anything. Men were compelled to sail in ships which were bound to founder if a storm came. Samuel Plimsoll was determined to do something about this, although he realised there was fierce opposition from powerful men to whom this iniquitous procedure brought a great deal of wealth. Plimsoll found it difficult to know how and where to begin to make a significant step to combat this injustice. He decided it needed to be done through parliament, and was elected an MP in 1868. He got the ear of Benjamin Disraeli who promised in 1875 (seven years later!) to introduce a bill to put things right. The wealthy ship-owners, however, applied such pressure that the bill had to be withdrawn. Plimsoll, in his frustration, lost his temper and called the House of Commons, the Prime Minister, and the offending ship-owners a set of villains. Public interest had now been raised and the pressure of public opinion became greater than the pressure of wealthy vested interest, and the bill was eventually passed in 1876. The Plimsoll line – a mark on a ship which must never be submerged beneath the water as a result of the weight that it carries – has become standard. Eight years is a long time to fight in parliament. Eight years is a long time to keep pressing on in a battle which seemed so constantly hopeless, so strong were the forces on the other side. It was sheer persistence which did it, founded on Plimsoll's conviction that what he was doing was just and necessary. The Plimsoll line is Samuel Plimsoll's memorial today; a memorial to a heart and spirit which refused to give up until the difficulties were overcome.

So it must ever be with forgiveness – we must keep on even when our emotions and our memories betray us!

Live the gospel
Perhaps the most powerful weapon in the Christian armoury is a new and living appreciation of the gospel in a deeply personal way. One of the keystones in the apostle Paul's teaching is that every Christian without exception

is 'in Christ'. This oft-repeated little phrase signifies something of the essence of Paul's gospel. Watchman Nee uses an illustration that if I put a dollar note between the pages of a magazine and then burn the magazine, the dollar note suffers the same fate as the magazine – it ends up amongst the pile of ashes as ashes itself. So it is that, just as effectively, God has put us in Christ. What happened to him happened also to us. All the experiences he met, we too have met *in him*. So it is that Paul cries, '. . . we know that our old being has been put to death with Christ on his cross, in order that the power of the sinful self might be destroyed, so that we should no longer be the slaves of sin' (Romans 6:6). This is the reverse of *our* struggling to achieve something. Paul is referring to history, our history, written in Christ before we were born. The glorious truth is that our crucifixion with Christ is an historic fact. Our deliverance from sin is based, not on what we can do, nor even on what God is going to do for us, but on what he has already done for us in Christ. When that reality dawns on us, and we begin to learn how to rest in it (ie 'In the same way you are to think of yourselves as dead, so far as sin is concerned, but living in fellowship with God through Christ Jesus' [Romans 6:11]), then we have discovered the secret of a holy life and the means whereby we are able to lay hold, at last, of an elusive forgiveness of others.

If someone slanders you, misrepresents you, is falsely critical of you, and in your presence wounds you, how do you meet the situation? As a Christian you steel yourself, compress your lips, clench your teeth, swallow hard, and take a firm grip on yourself. If with a great effort and exercise of will you manage to suppress all sign of resentment and give a reasonably gentle answer in return, you feel you have succeeded in showing a Christian response and have gained a significant spiritual victory. Unhappily, the resentment is still there; it has merely been pushed down and covered up. It only requires the right set of circumstances, the right climate, the right company, and sometimes the right pressure of provocation for the whole thing to surface – often in an explosive way. The problem lies in attempting to do for God what only God can do (and has done) for you. The secret of deliverance from sin, even the sin of unforgiveness, is not to do something, but to trust and rest in what God has done for you.

Watchman Nee tells (in *Sit, Walk, Stand*, Kingsway) of an engineer who had left his homeland because of his employment. He was away for two or three years, and during his absence his wife was unfaithful to him and went off with one of his best friends. On his return home he found he had lost his wife, his two children and his best friend. 'At the close of a meeting I was addressing,' writes Watchman Nee, 'this grief-stricken man unburdened himself to me. "Day and night for two solid years my heart has been full of hatred," he said. "I am a Christian, and I know I ought to forgive my wife and my friend, but though I try and try to forgive them, I simply cannot. Every day I resolve to love them, and every day I fail. What can I do about it?" "Do nothing at all," I replied. "What do you mean?" he asked, startled. "Am I to continue to hate them?" So I explained: "The solution of your problem lies here, that when the Lord Jesus died on the Cross He not only bore your sins away, but He bore YOU away too. When He was crucified, your old man was crucified in Him, so that that unforgiving 'you', who simply cannot love those who have wronged you, has been taken right out of the way in His death. God has dealt with the whole situation in the Cross, and there is nothing left for you to deal with. Just say to Him, 'Lord, I cannot love and I give up trying, but I count on Thy perfect love. I cannot forgive, but I trust Thee to forgive instead of me, and to do so henceforth in me.' "

The man sat there amazed and said, "That's all so new, I feel I must DO something about it." Then a moment later he added again, "But what can I DO?" "God is waiting until you cease to do," I said. "When you cease doing then God will begin. Have you ever tried to save a drowning man? The trouble is that his fear prevents him trusting himself to you. When that is so, there are just two ways of going about it. Either you must knock him unconscious and then drag him to the shore, or else you must leave him to struggle until his strength gives way before you go to his rescue. If you try to save him while he has any strength left, he will clutch at you in his terror, and drag you under, and both he and you will be lost. God is waiting for your store of strength to be utterly exhausted before He can deliver you. Once you have ceased to struggle, He will do everything. God is waiting for you to despair." '

Watchman Nee continues, 'My engineer friend jumped up. "Brother," he said, "I've seen it. Praise God, it's all right with me now! There's nothing for me to do. HE has done it all!" And with radiant face he went off rejoicing.'

That is a good account of a practical handling of a very familiar situation. In the last analysis we can confront the reality of our resentment and hurt; we can separate the wrong-doer from the wrong he has done and see the person who really lives beneath the cloak of his wrong-doing; by an act of our will we can let the past, with all its pain, consciously go rather than holding on to it tightly; we can keep working at the reality of forgiving; but until we learn the principle of the exchanged life in and with Christ the conflict will rage without satisfactory result.

Bernard Shaw saw forgiveness as weakness and called it 'a beggar's refuge', but he was wrong. It is not weakness and fantasy, but strength and reality. Vengeance can never even the score, no matter how convinced we are that it does. Vengeance ties the injured and the injurer to an endless escalation of retaliation. Mahatma Ghandi once said that if we all live by an 'eye for an eye' kind of justice, the whole world will be blind. He was right. Reinhold Niebuhr, the theologian, saw this after World War II when he said, 'We must finally be reconciled with our foe, lest we both perish in the vicious circle of hatred.'

Forgiveness breaks pain's grip on our minds and opens the door to a new beginning.

In co-operating with God in forgiveness we have the joy of coming as close as any human being can to the essentially divine act of creation. We heal damage that has been done and create a new beginning out of past pain. 'All you need to do', my young paper-folding friend said to me, 'is to follow the instructions carefully and you'll see it works.' When I tried, and it didn't, with a natural child-like straightforwardness he said, 'You need to keep trying.' So it is with forgiveness – we need to keep at it. The prize for winning through is indispensable – for us and for others.

4

Seventy times seven

Most Christians can manage to see clearly the need for forgiveness and respond to the command to forgive even when it hurts. Where most struggle is with the need to go on forgiving. It is never easy to say to the same person who persistently wrongs you, 'I forgive you' – and mean it! Something instinctively says within us: 'This cannot be right.' Anger, bitterness, self-pity, accusations of weakness all follow one on top of the other when we are required to forgive again . . . and again.

I was a new young minister in Dumbarton when Joan came to see me. She had been married for nineteen years and had a fine teenage son. She was a happy, archetypal mum. She had a warm, outgoing, generous disposition and appeared to be the kind of person who would be easy to live with. Her son, Richard, was of the same disposition as his mother – friendly, co-operative and easy to talk to. The morning she appeared on my doorstep, however, I knew there was something seriously wrong. As soon as she came into my home she wept. Then the story came out. Her husband, who did not share her new-found faith in Christ, was a compulsive gambler. He was a reserved, shy man who appeared to have few, if any, really close friends. On the face of it he seemed agreeable and reasonable. His conversation was gentle and understanding. He was certainly not an aggressive, domineering personality; but he gambled! He worked in the local shipyard in a noisy, dirty job where he 'finished off' the rivets that bound together the massive sheets of steel on the ship. It was hard work and he earned good money. In the days when Denny's shipyard was fully operational there seemed all the ingredients for a happy marriage, a secure home life and a fulfilling social life; but he gambled!

Many a Friday evening he came home minus the contents of his whole wage-packet. Long years before he had run out of excuses like, 'It was stolen!' or, 'I lost it on the way home!' The truth was known. Cards, horses, dogs, anything got the benefit of his money. He would never have dreamt of stealing from anyone – except Joan and their home. All that she ever possessed or that he had ever given her had long since gone, and lies and deceit were a way of life with Joan so far as Jack was concerned. She had had to move out of their home to safeguard a roof over her head for herself and her little boy. The home that she had made was a warm, friendly, comfortable place up an outside stairway in the oldest part of the town. It in many ways was an extension of Joan's personality.

So the story came out on that late winter morning. Money was tight, young Richard had financial needs that Joan could no longer meet (he was talking about getting married), and Jack was asking to join them and begin again. I felt every single day of my inexperience and immaturity. Joan was not the complaining sort, but she had shared the situation so that I could properly understand, and give her some direction. After all, she was a very young Christian and I was wearing a clerical collar. All that was in her longed for a secure family life with her husband and son. She loved Jack and wept over his weaknesses with great sobs. All that was in me said that she had been deceived, misled, let down, the recipient of tearful promises from Jack that he would never gamble again if she would have him back – but he always did – and so she mustn't be so foolish again.

However, I knew the clear teaching of Jesus on forgiveness. Somehow it seemed so much easier to stand in a pulpit and preach with great conviction and clarity what the Bible said than it did to talk quietly with Joan about it. Wasn't it Peter who asked Jesus, 'Lord, if my brother keeps on sinning against me, how many times do I have to forgive him? Seven times?' To which Jesus gave the astonishing reply, 'No, not seven times, but seventy times seven.'

A pointed parable

Peter asked his question, but immediately gave his own answer. No doubt Peter was struggling with a very personal issue at this time and wanted Jesus to affirm that he was doing right. Peter, as a well-brought up Jew, knew the clear rabbinic teaching on forgiveness. Rabbi Jose ben Hanina said, 'He who begs forgiveness from his neighbour must not do so more than three times.' So what Peter, who never seemed to do anything by half, had done was to take the rabbinic limit of forgiveness, multiply it by two and add one for good measure, and then sit back smugly. Maybe Peter had forgiven someone seven times and felt it likely there would be an eighth time, and he wanted to be sure he had Jesus' approval to withhold forgiveness. He did not get it! Instead he provoked a parable from Jesus about a servant who himself was forgiven an enormous debt; and who went out and dealt mercilessly with a fellow servant who owed him a debt which was an infinitesimal fraction of what he himself had owed. For his mercilessness the unforgiving servant was utterly condemned (Matthew 18:21–35).

The bones of the story are clear and the message penetratingly simple. A king was putting his affairs in order and decided to check on his servants' accounts. He discovered an enormous piece of embezzlement. Perhaps the unforgiving servant was the one whose debt prompted the king's investigation. After all, ten thousand talents must have made quite a difference in the king's bank statement. The king's reaction was swift and clear – the servant was to be jailed and his wife, family, and assets were all to be sold as part-payment for his debt and folly. (A talent in today's currency would be well in excess of £500, so the debt he owed would be over five million pounds!) However, the whole point of the story is not the exact sum, but the fact that the servant's debt was totally unpayable.

Equally incredible was the king's response to the passionate pleading of the servant for mercy. Political leaders at that time were not noted for their clemency. However, the king behaved in a remarkably compassionate way. He forgave the servant and released him. It is difficult for us in our somewhat more humanitarian society to appreciate the impact this would have had on Jesus' hearers. But it seems that the forgiven servant immediately went out and found one of his fellow servants who owed him one hundred denarii – a matter of a few pounds. He would not listen to the reasonable request for time to pay. He had his fellow servant prosecuted, condemned and punished according to the law.

The other servants were so outraged by the sheer thankless injustice of the whole affair that they went and reported the incident to the king. The king acted immediately and affirmed that mercy received should have stimulated mercy given – the forgiven need to forgive! The king withdrew his mercy and demanded justice until the debt had been discharged. Because the debt was unpayable it meant that punishment could never be lifted, and justice rather than mercy would reign for the remainder of the man's life.

Such love!
The story is full of vivid touches. Not least is the wide difference between the two debts. The servant was owed approximately one five-hundred-thousandth of what he

himself owed the king. The contrast between the two debts is staggering; they cannot be compared. The whole thrust of this is that no matter how badly we have been wounded and maligned by others it can never compare with what we have done to God; and if God has forgiven the debt we owe him, we must unconditionally forgive the debts others owe us. Nothing that we have to forgive can even faintly compare with what we have been forgiven. Our pride and self-satisfaction make it difficult for us to appreciate the nature of our sin and what it has done and continues to do to a holy God. We may be willing to acknowledge that we are by no means perfect, but at the same time be unable to appreciate the sinfulness of the sin in our hearts. Perhaps Wesley touched reality when he sang:

> Not the labour of my hands
> Can fulfil Thy law's demand;
> Could my zeal no respite know,
> Could my tears forever flow,
> All for sin could not atone . . .

We have been forgiven a debt which is beyond all paying: forgiven because of what God has done for us in his Son on the cross. There alone can we begin to appreciate the nature of sin – it slew the sinless, perfect Son of God – and the true nature of forgiveness.

Double standards!

Another vivid touch in the story is that the forgiven servant 'grabbed and started choking' his fellow servant. This is a reference to an ancient practice. In Roman times the custom was to grasp a debtor by the neck of his toga and rush him half-throttled and gasping to court. The Greek custom was similar since in the ancient world the plaintiff often made his own arrests. The Greeks actually talked about choking the life out of a debtor when they meant dragging him to court. More significant still, however, is that in Matthew 18:28 'Pay back what you owe me' has no 'me' in the original Greek text. In other words it is a perfectly general command: 'Pay your debts!' It is as if at the end of a long argument with many demands and answering pleadings, the discussion was ended by the unforgiving servant saying pompously and self-righteously, 'Any honest man pays his debts.' There is something almost comical, if it were not so despicable, about a man who had just failed to pay an enormous and unpayable debt which ran into millions affirming to a man who owed him a few pounds that honest men pay their debts!

Of all human faults that of having double standards is probably the most common. Often we are critical in others of the very thing that we are easy on with ourselves. Often our eyes see clearly what is wrong in others, but they are blind to our own faults. What is thrift in us is meanness in others. What is frankness in us is aggressive insensitivity in others. What are reasons for us are excuses in others. Here is a man who laid down categorically, as a universal law, that honest men pay their debts, whilst he himself was quite willing to accept the cancelling of the enormous debt which he owed. How important for him, and for us, to receive Jesus' commandment to do to others as we would have them do to us. If we treated others with the same tenderness, understanding and sympathy with which we consider ourselves it would be a much happier world and much easier to live in.

The crunch

The main teaching of Jesus' story is that our willingness to forgive others has a direct bearing on God's forgiveness of us. The whole parable is really a commentary on two clear teachings of Jesus. Way back at the beginning of Jesus' ministry he had gathered his disciples around him and he had shared his 'manifesto' of the kingdom of God with them (Matthew 5–7). Almost at the beginning of the 'manifesto' he said, 'Happy are those who are merciful to others; God will be merciful to them' (Matthew 5:7). Later on he said, 'This is how you should pray: . . . Forgive us the wrongs we have done, as we forgive the wrongs others have done to us.' Never do we demonstrate the Christian dynamic more clearly than when we forgive.

It seems to be true that God's inflow of mercy to us coincides with our outflow of mercy to others. The prayer which Jesus taught the disciples is frighteningly direct. 'Forgive us', Jesus taught, 'as we forgive.' The implication is that we ask God to forgive us in proportion as we forgive others. This is the only part of the prayer which Jesus picks out for comment later on. 'If you forgive others the wrongs they have done to you, your Father in heaven will also forgive you,' he said. 'But if you do not forgive others, then your Father will not forgive the wrongs you have done.'

I could not get this out of my mind as Joan sat there that morning. It is so much easier to give counsel and guidance to others than to receive it for yourself. I hesitated because I knew the awful struggle I would have if the roles were reversed and I were in her shoes. Yet, as ever, it is not the parts of the Bible which I don't understand which bother me, but the parts of the Bible which I do understand. Surely Jesus was saying that when we pray this prayer for forgiveness and yet harbour bitterness in our hearts, we are quite deliberately asking God *not* to forgive us, because we ourselves are not really forgiving others.

. . . as we forgive . . .

Every morning in his South Sea home, Robert Louis Stevenson used to conduct family worship. One morning in the middle of the Lord's Prayer he suddenly rose from his knees and left the room. His wife was alarmed because he had very indifferent health and she thought he had fallen ill. When she found him she asked what was wrong with him. To her great surprise he said, 'I'm not fit to pray the Lord's Prayer today.' No doubt there were issues he had to resolve and conflicts he had to settle: someone he needed to contact in order to put things right. How important it is for us to pray not only with faith, but also with honesty. We need to remember that to know the freedom and peace of forgiveness we need ourselves to forgive.

Why should this be? On the face of it there seems to be a condition which we must meet in order to receive grace, and that is a denial of what we understand grace to be. On the face of it there seems to be an element of bargaining in God's dealing with us. Why this clear insistence by God that in order to enjoy the reality of being a forgiven man I need to accept the responsibility of forgiving? There can only be one reason for that. It is not possible for people to experience close and meaningful fellowship if they do not share the same mind, heart and spirit. It is possible to be close friends with someone whose opinions I do not share. I have found, increasingly as the years have passed, that it is wonderfully possible to have real fellowship without compromising convictions which are deeply held. But if our fundamental outlook on life, on the world, and on people generally is quite different then there can be no deep relationship or friendship. In other words relationships depend on sharing a basic philosophy of life. This applies to God and us. If we see things in a fundamentally different way from God then inevitably there can be no fellowship between us. God's whole attitude is one of forgiving love to the undeserving and the unlovely. He sends his rain on the just and the unjust and makes his sunshine warm the evil and the good. The whole drama of redemption is a demonstration of this. He sent his own dearly beloved Son into history because of his active outgoing love. In Jesus God does more than wait for us to come humbly and contritely back to him begging his forgiveness, he goes, out of his own loving will, to find us and offer his love. He takes the initiative.

At the famous Glenalmond School in Scotland, there stands a memorial to Alexander Cumine Russell. Soon after Russell left Glenalmond School, he became an officer in the Highland Light Infantry. His regiment was on the HMS *Birkenhead* when she sank. The women were ordered to the boats. When one of these boats was filled, the captain of the *Birkenhead* placed Russell in charge of it with orders to allow nobody else to get on board. Just as the boat was pulling away from the doomed ship, a man who had been struggling in the water grasped one of the oars and pulled himself to a position in which everyone aboard the lifeboat could see his face. A piercing scream rent the air: 'Save him! He's my husband!' a woman cried. Without a moment's hesitation, Alexander Cumine Russell leapt overboard, helped the man into the boat and was seen no more. He had disobeyed his orders, but he had responded instinctively to something which clearly was in the heart of Jesus – he saved others at the cost of his own life.

Any illustration of what God has done for us in his Son, Jesus Christ, must of necessity be limited. Russell's heroic act does not match the deliberate, premeditated act of God that sent his Son into the world to redeem mankind. This was no afterthought, this was pre-ordained from before the foundation of the world. God is love, and his love means the offer of complete forgiveness. So it is inevitable that if we are dominated by resentment, and coldness of heart, and bitterness of spirit; if in our hearts there is built a little chapel of hate to which we go from time to time; if we say, 'I can never forgive and I will never forget,' then our basic attitude to life is radically and diametrically opposed to all that God is.

Jesus' teaching on forgiveness shows that in order to share fellowship we need to share a fundamental attitude and direction of life. A God whose being is grace can only enter fully into a living relationship with those whose attitude – however imperfect their activity might be – is gracious. The whole emphasis of Jesus' teaching is that what we *are* always comes before what we *do*. This, of course, is the antithesis of the non-Christian view of

Christianity. If you were to ask a non-Christian what a Christian is he would normally reply in terms of what he understands a Christian is supposed to *do*, or not to do. But Jesus teaches that what we *do* springs from what we *are*. The important priority is to attend to and shape our character, and our conduct will follow on from that naturally. Jesus in his 'manifesto of the kingdom' – the Sermon on the Mount – is not instructing his disciples how to work *for* their salvation, but rather how to work *out* their salvation. Christianity begins with belief and trust before it tackles behaviour (although it affirms that behaviour must always be the inevitable consequence of belief). It was John Calvin who said, 'While it is faith alone that justifies, the faith that justifies is never alone.' In other words, faith must always be accompanied by doing and obedience. Jesus in the Sermon on the Mount clearly answers the question, 'What is the good life?' What he said is different from anything anybody ever had said before or has said since.

There are three basic answers to the question. First of all there are those who clearly believe that the good life is to be found in what we *have*. For them the top values are wealth, health, friends and faculties. Then there are those who have concluded that the good life is to be found in what you *do*. For them the absorbing interest of life is the hobby which occupies them or the amount of travel they are able to get in without neglecting other responsibilities. However, Jesus quite clearly affirms that the good life is really to be found in what we *are*. The real world that I live in is not the world outside, but the world inside. The great challenge which faces us is not the conquest of outer space, but the conquest of inner space. The ingredients of Christian character are noted by Jesus in Matthew 5:1–12.

True mercy

So it is that a forgiving God can only really enter into significant fellowship with those whose hearts are open to forgive. A merciful God can only really enter into significant fellowship with those who show mercy to others (Matthew 5:7). This has nothing to do with a bargaining God, but rather with the being of God. What does it mean to be merciful? It is a thing of the heart. It has to do with my attitude towards a person or circumstances. It is to feel compassion for someone who is in need of one kind or another. It is also a thing of the will. Mercy is not a passive, emotional thing – it has to do with doing something about how you feel. It has to do with responding relevantly to the need which has stirred your emotions. But mercy primarily has to do with the mind.

In Luke 10:25–37 Jesus tells the story of the good Samaritan. The whole point of the parable is that the one who responded to the need of the man in the ditch was a Samaritan. The racial barrier between the Jew and the Samaritan was as great as any racial barrier has ever been in history. The reason why the Jew was going down the road from Jerusalem to Jericho is that he was avoiding going through Samaria. He was on his way, no doubt, to Galilee and would not dream of going through Samaria no matter how inconvenient and dangerous the alternative might be. The implication of the story is heightened by the fact that the other Jews (ie the priest and the Levite) were indifferent to the plight of one of their own kinsmen – presumably because they were too intent on their religious responsibilities which they saw as pleasing God. Jesus here is laying down clearly the truth that mercy is so much in the heart of God that merciful attitudes and activities are of much more value to him than precise and punctilious religious observances. So, in the parable, it was the Samaritan who stopped, acted, and showed mercy.

Mercy is shown in its true colours when the act is done for the ungrateful and the entirely undeserving. This is so much akin to the nature and heart of God as he has revealed himself in the Bible, and even more plainly and powerfully in his Son, our Lord Jesus Christ. This is the

whole thrust of the story of the good Samaritan. The
Samaritan knew he would be unlikely to be thanked for
what he had done. This quality is so dear to the heart of
God. This alone explains the sole commentary on the
Lord's Prayer given by Jesus – that our forgiveness
depends on our forgiving. Jesus is referring not to the
grounds of our salvation, but indicating the grounds of
real communion and fellowship with God. In fact it is
only when we are living under the sheer undeserved generosity of God that we can show mercy.

Again and again . . .
When Joan come to me that morning in Dumbarton years
ago, I advised her to forgive Jack, yet again, and have
him back. To begin all over again, aware of the risk that
he would not keep his promises or fulfil his commitment
to her. For her to fail to forgive would seem to fly in the
face of God's revealed, clear word and lose the reality
and spontancity of her fellowship with him.

Joan did have Jack back, and for a while all was well.
The family was united. Everyone seemed happy. Jack
apparently was keeping his word, and with a fair bit of
support (maybe not as much as it needed to be from the
church) he kept off gambling. However, the weeks rolled
into months, and people around him began to find there
were other responsibilities that absorbed their attention
and claimed their time. The support, such as it was, was
withdrawn (and I suspect that the fellowship of the church
did not continue to pray as they had been doing) and Jack
was back gambling again. So we entered once more into
answering the question: 'What now?' There is only one
answer to that question – difficult and demanding as it is
– and that is 'forgive him'. When I left Dumbarton the
same situation was still being worked through.

Most of us are 489 people. If the standard of Jesus is
that we are to forgive seventy times seven, am I then
entitled to withhold forgiveness when I have been wronged seventy times seven plus one? Of course that was

never Jesus' intention. Seventy times seven was a figure that Jesus plucked out of the air. He is really saying, 'You must forgive and go on forgiving. It is useless to go on counting the number of times you have been wronged and need to forgive.'

'I wish I could say', writes Corrie ten Boom (in *Tramp for the Lord*), 'that after a long and fruitful life, travelling the world, I had learned to forgive all my enemies. I wish I could say that merciful and charitable thoughts just naturally flowed from me and on to others. But they don't. If there is one thing that I have learned since I've passed my eightieth birthday, it's that I can't store up good feelings and behaviour – but only draw them fresh from God each day.'

Corrie confesses that maybe it is better that way since every time she went to God he taught her something else. She recalls how when she was almost seventy years of age some loved and trusted Christian friends did something which hurt her deeply. She felt that having confronted the awful bitterness in her heart over her imprisonment in Ravensbruck concentration camp, where her sister Betsie died through malnutrition, forgiving Christian friends would not be all that difficult. It was not so. For weeks she seethed inside. She testifies that she asked God again to work his miracle in her – and again it happened. First the clinical decision; then the flood of joy and peace. Forgiveness had been released and she was restored into fellowship once more with her heavenly Father.

To her astonishment one night she was suddenly awake in the middle of the night going through the whole affair again in its finest detail. 'These were my friends,' she thought. 'These were people I loved. If it had been strangers, I wouldn't have minded so.' She sat up and switched on the light. 'Father, I thought it was all forgiven. Please help me do it.' To her dismay the same thing happened during the following night. They talked so sweetly too! Never a hint of what they were planning. 'Father!' She cried in alarm. 'Help me!'

It was under this pressure that Corrie ten Boom learned another secret of God's forgiveness. It is not enough to say simply, 'I forgive you.' We must then begin to live it out. In her case, that meant acting as though their sins, like hers, were buried in the depths of the deepest sea. If God could remember them no more – and that is what he said – then neither could she. She concluded that the reason the hurtful thoughts kept coming back to her was that she kept turning the wrong that had been done to her over in her mind.

So she discovered another of God's principles; we can trust God not only for our emotions, but also for our thoughts. She affirms that she asked God to renew her mind, and he also took away her thoughts. She tells how God had still more to teach her through this episode. Many years later, after she had passed her eightieth birthday, an American friend came to visit her in Holland. As they sat in her little apartment in Baarn he asked her about those people from long ago who had taken advantage of her.

'It's nothing,' she said a little smugly, 'It is all forgiven.'

'By you, yes,' he said. 'But what about them? Have they accepted your forgiveness?'

'They say there is nothing to forgive! They deny it ever happened. No matter what they say, though, I can prove they were wrong.' She went eagerly to her desk. 'See, I have it in black and white! I saved all their letters and I can show you where . . .'

'Corrie!' Her friend slipped his arm through hers and gently closed the drawer. 'Aren't you the one whose sins are at the bottom of the sea? Yet are the sins of your friends etched in black and white?'

For an astonishing moment she discovered that she could not find her voice – convicted, shocked, disturbed. At last she whispered, 'Lord Jesus, who takes all my sins away, forgive me for preserving all these years the evidence against others! Give me grace to burn all the blacks and whites as a sweet-smelling sacrifice to your glory.'

Corrie did not go to sleep that night until she gone through the desk and pulled out those letters, curling now with age, and fed them into her little coal-burning grate. As the flames leaped and glowed, so did her heart. 'Forgive us our trespasses,' she recalled that Jesus had taught us, 'as we forgive those that trespass against us.' In the ashes of those letters she was seeing yet another facet of the mercy of God. She wondered, although now an octogenarian, what more God would teach her about forgiveness in the years that still lay ahead. She did not then know, but for the present she was content with the good news of that night. She comments that, 'Forgiveness is the key which unlocks the door of resentment and the handcuffs of hatred. It breaks the chains of bitterness and the shackles of selfishness.'

The forgiveness of Jesus not only takes away our sins perfectly, however many they are and however often we have had to come to him in confession and penitence, but it also makes them as if they had never been. Realising this and receiving it gives us the motivation and the foundation by which we can release others in forgiveness, no matter how much or how often they have wronged us. This is so different from the Pharisaical, self-righteous legalism that keeps a score of wrong – four hundred and eighty-five, four hundred and eighty-six, four hundred and eighty-seven, four hundred and eighty-eight, and still counting!

5

Dare to discipline

Forgiveness is dangerous. It's vital, but it's dangerous. And it's dangerous because a sloppy approach to forgiveness may encourage carelessness (by those who feel they can get away with anything) and irresponsibility (by those who would rather not face the difficult task of exercising fair and godly discipline). Yet an undisciplined household will always be an unhappy household. To allow everybody to please themselves and do whatever they like may seem liberal and generous, but it results in sadness, confusion and insecurity. Someone once said that 'a man's real difficulties begin when he is free to do what he likes.' That certainly was true in the case of the prodigal son (Luke 15). So deeply did he learn the lesson that unbridled freedom was destructive and unsatisfying that he returned to the structured discipline of his father's house, preferring the lot of one of the hired servants there to the free life of 'the far country'.

In family life the child who has everything done for him, everything given to him, and little or nothing required of him, is a deprived child. A family doctor writing in a national periodical once said that it is like serving a child a diet without the essential vitamins and minerals . . . and he will shortly show signs of nutritional deficiency. 'A home that has no taboos, that makes no demands, that requires no politeness or conformity, that sets no firm rules or limits, is a home that the city sanitary inspector ought to serve a ticket to,' he writes. 'It's an unhealthy place, a breeding ground for trouble. And trouble there will be. A child's character needs adequate structure, and to begin with these controls must come from without. Only when the external controls have been adequate can the child take them into himself, make them part of himself, and thus have the necessary internal structure to allow growth to proceed fully and well.'

The parent who tries to please the child by giving in to him and expecting nothing from him ends up by pleasing no one, least of all the child. For in the end, when trouble results, the child will blame the parent for his gutlessness.

As it is in the human family, so it is in the family of God. More than 300 years ago John Calvin reminded us:

> . . . if no society, indeed no house which has even a small family, can be kept in proper condition without discipline, it is much more necessary in the church, whose condition should be as ordered as possible.

That discipline is necessary in the church is not often questioned. But the form, the direction, the course of action, the short-term and long-range objectives do raise questions that need to be answered, however awkward, embarrassing and painful that may be. We noted earlier that forgetting is not a prerequisite to perfect forgiveness; we need also to understand that discipline is not a contradiction of, nor a barrier to, perfect forgiveness. Discipline and forgiveness are not mutually exclusive.

But why write on church discipline in a book on forgiveness? The answer to that question has to do with the difference between forgiveness and restoration. Forgiveness can be both given and received in a moment: but restoration, which is the rebuilding – following forgiveness – of broken relationships, normally takes a bit longer.

The consequences of wrong within a corporate setting take time to unravel and the unravelling and 'repair' require patience and humility to achieve. What will, almost always, come to light is the need for discipline. The willingness to face this will bring rich rewards.

But isn't church discipline a matter for leaders alone? No. It is for leaders, first of all, so that those who have responsibility for local church leadership can reflect on it and take Biblical action. But this chapter is for all, so that those who comprise the membership of the local church can reflect on its contents with a view to Biblical understanding. Both action and understanding are necessary to enable discipline to operate in the right climate, and to achieve results which are healing and restorative rather than damaging and divisive.

Church discipline

The Bible commands discipline among the people of God. Discipline is not an option, but an obligation. To shrink from discipline may well be understandable, but it is disobedience to do so.

Jesus, as he begins the final six months of his earthly ministry, gives a very clear, practical directive in Matthew 18:15–17. Discipline begins by honest and accurate confrontation: 'If your brother sins against you, go to him and show him his fault.' When we are aware that wrong has been done, we need to put our complaint into words. The worst thing we can do about a wrong is to brood about it. Any such feeling needs to be brought into the open, faced, and stated. Sometimes, though not always, the very stating of it will show how relatively unimportant and trivial the whole thing is. The wrong-doer has the right, however, to be confronted by his offence – otherwise discipline is unjust and destructive. Jesus implies that this confrontation needs to be done privately and personally. More trouble has been caused in the church by the writing of letters than by almost anything else. A letter can often be cold, clinical and impersonal. It can so easily be misread or misunderstood. The tone of a letter often comes from the heart of the reader rather than from the heart of the writer. 'Go to him,' Jesus counsels, and deal with the matter face to face. The spoken word can often settle a difference which the written word would only exacerbate.

Jesus then prescribed the course of action should the initial discussion produce no response. The final action to be taken if there is still no response from the wrong-doer is that he will be excluded from the church and disregarded as a member of the family of God: '. . . treat him as though he were a pagan or a tax collector.' This is a very clear and strong directive from Jesus that any situation in which there is a breach of personal relationships within the Christian community can never be tolerated.

Discipline in the early church

The unfolding and exhilarating life of the early church was not undisciplined. Luke describes that first Christian community in Acts 4:32–35. Having done that he unveils its imperfection in the story of Ananias and Sapphira (Acts 5:1–11). Ananias and Sapphira lied to the church; and as a result, they died. This story shocks many, who feel that the punishment does not fit the crime – it is far too severe. It is never easy for us to grasp how different God's priorities and appraisal are from ours – the things we regard as small, God regards as big; and often the things we regard as big, God regards as small.

One of the keys to understanding the story of Ananias and Sapphira is that for the first time in the Acts of the Apostles the world 'church' occurs. The whole section can never be understood until we have a right concept of two things, God and the church. God is concerned that the church has far more to fear from corruption within than from opposition without. Jesus regarded hypocrisy as the most damaging and destructive thing of all. If allowed to go unchecked it would cause the collapse of the whole church. So discipline is devastatingly swift. Acts 5:1–11 illustrates how seriously God regards sin within the church and the pressing need to deal with it.

This need for discipline continues in the instruction (recorded in the New Testament letters) given to the early church. The early church was like a little island surrounded by a sea of paganism. It was difficult for new-born Christians to unlearn the practices which generations of loose-living had made part of their lives. Yet if the church was to remain strong and effective it needed to guard its purity. In sexual matters, for example, the pagan world did not know the meaning of chastity. It was enormously hard for the Christian church to escape infection. As then, so it is becoming today!

In the church at Corinth a specific case of blatant immorality was being accepted and tolerated by the church. A man was in an immoral relationship with his own stepmother. This was not only forbidden by Jewish law (Leviticus 18:8), but was abhorred by the heathen (1 Corinthians 5:1–5). Paul clearly is not only shocked by the sin, but is also shocked by the church's attitude to the sinner. An easy-going attitude to sin is always dangerous.

Perhaps our greatest security against sin lies in our being shocked and disgusted by it. It was Thomas Carlyle who once said that men must see the infinite beauty of holiness and the infinite damnability of sin. It is not a question of being critical and condemnatory, but it is a question of grasping fully what sin did to Jesus Christ, God's only Son, and what sin continues to do to ordinary men and women like us. No Christian can ever regard sin lightly or take an easy-going view of it.

Paul writes to the Corinthians that this sin must be recognised and the sinner needs to be disciplined. In the event of persistent, unrepentant sin, the church is to be sad – and the word which Paul uses for grief here is the word which is used for mourning for the dead. This is not self-righteousness, but the picture of an individual or a community that is humbled. In this attitude the sinner needs to be confronted honestly and courageously and, if he remains unrepentant, expelled.

Instructions for spiritual maturity

Yet another example of instruction given to the early church is towards the end of the first letter to the Thessalonian Christians, where Paul urgently and concisely gives fifteen instructions for spiritual maturity and wholeness within the church (1 Thessalonians 5:12–18). Amongst them is an urgent command to 'warn the idle' (v 14). We are certainly not to turn a blind eye to those who are not behaving properly within the fellowship. A mature church is one where wrong is righted, error is challenged and discipline is exercised.

A concern for discipline is evident in Paul's pastoral writing to Timothy: 'rebuke publicly all those who commit sins, so that the rest may be afraid' (1 Timothy 5:20). Those who are wise in leadership will know when it is right to expose and when it is right to take a quieter and more secret route. Whatever happens, however, the church must never condone sin. In the end, discipline is not simply for the spiritual health and growth of individuals, but will have a profound effect on the honour, integrity and credibility of the gospel.

A note in Paul's letter to Titus (Titus 1:10–16) contains similar instructions. The concern of this letter is that clear, sound doctrine will lead to good deeds, and chapter one is all about sound doctrine leading to good deeds in the church. Paul is deeply disturbed that interesting, and often convincing, false teachers were getting into the church and causing confusion over law and grace and tradition and truth. These false teachers were to be rebuked 'sharply' (v 13), with severity. They were to be confronted and dealt with in an uncompromising way.

In this same practical, pastoral letter Paul gives simple and clear instructions as he concludes. Paul knew the tendency of the Greeks to spend their time on fine-spun hypothetical problems. He was even more aware of the Jewish rabbis spending their time building up imaginary and edifying genealogies for the characters of the Old Testament. Paul calls such people 'divisive', since they spend their time arguing for the sake of arguing about points which don't even matter! Paul commands that the divisive be admonished: 'give at least two warnings to the person who causes divisions, and then have nothing more to do with him. You know that such a person is corrupt, and his sins prove that he is wrong.' Having given suitable confrontation and exercised godly patience, discipline is to be implemented for the sake of the health and effectiveness of the whole body of Christ.

In the last book of the Bible the risen Christ calls the churches (addressed in Revelation 2 and 3) to repentance, and warns solemnly of impending discipline if his words are ignored. However we may insist otherwise, love is not blind. In fact love has a way of opening our eyes to the true nature of the situation and causing us to take action which we would rather avoid, but realising all the while that the most unloving thing is to do nothing about it. In these Bible passages God makes it abundantly clear that he intends the church to take corrective measures in the event of its members persisting in sin. Whatever our reluctance might be it is irresponsible to cast aside disciplining in the light of these biblical admonitions.

Some very clear features emerge from all that we have explored in scripture. First of all we need to see again that God is more sensitive to sin than we are – presumably because he is more aware than we are of the infinite and eternal havoc it can cause. Secondly, confrontation of the sinner with his sin is God's way of dealing with it. So we are encouraged that this, too, should be our way of dealing with it. The best method of doing this is verbal, face-to-face, personal confrontation. Thirdly, patience must always be exercised, as God has been so patient with every one of us. Damage can be caused by undue haste; and yet our patience must be without hesitancy or unrealistic delay. Fourthly, those who discipline must always do so with deep sadness of heart and humility of spirit. As we confront another with their sin it will always be with the awareness of how deeply this has cut into the person's life and how sore the heart of God is over it. It will always be with a deep consciousness that 'there, but for the grace of God, go I.'

An Edinburgh businessman had been prosecuted, found guilty and imprisoned for his offences against society. It caused a great stir throughout the city. Wide publicity had been added to his already heavy burden. The whole city was surprised and shocked at what had come to light. At that time a fine ministry was being exercised by the godly Dr Alexander Whyte in St George's West Church. The Sunday morning after these sad events, Alexander Whyte was standing in his vestry in the last moments before he went to lead his congregation in worship, and the church bells were ringing throughout the city calling the population to worship. Wistfully and sadly Whyte said to his colleague who was standing with him there in the vestry, 'He hears these same bells this morning in his prison cell in Saughton Prison – man, it might have been me!' At best all of us are simply sinners saved by the grace of God through faith.

Fifthly, where discipline is necessary there should be no hesitation about going public when appropriate. Finally, exclusion from the life and protection of the fellowship must result when there is no willingness to repent and change.

As I write these words I can feel a painful clutch at my own heart as I recall some instances through the years where discipline has had to be exercised. Discipline is never painless, but even if the method that was used and the way it was done may not always have been the best, the exercise of discipline seemed the right way to proceed. On reflection I think that the measures that were taken ought, often, to have been much more clearly defined, for the health of the body of Christ and for the future development of those who were disciplined.

The purpose of discipline

Discipline within the church has a number of purposes. Undoubtedly chief of these is that *obedience to the scriptures* is always right. We always honour God and exalt our Lord Jesus Christ when we act in obedience to the revealed will of God. God is not vindictive, but he is righteous and does not condone or compromise with sin. Then, secondly, there is clear evidence that the purpose of discipline is to *restore and benefit the offender*. However hard it is for us to receive the tougher parts of Matthew 18:15–17, the clear cry from Jesus' heart is that, 'If he listens to you, you have won your brother back.' Even in the vivid instance dealt with in Paul's first letter to the Corinthians (5:1–5) the concern was to bring the offender to his senses, and make him see the enormity of what he was doing. Discipline is exercised not solely to punish, but to awaken. On the unrepentant a verdict was not to be carried out with cold, sadistic cruelty, but rather in sorrow as for one who had died.

In the early church there was the conviction that punishment and discipline were for the making, not the breaking, of the person who sinned. Whatever to 'hand this man over to Satan' (1 Corinthians 5:15) may mean, the consequence of it is 'so that his spirit may be saved in the Day of the Lord.'

The short-term must always be seen in the light of the long-term, and the historical in the light of the eternal. In that marvellously tender passage towards the end of Paul's Galatian letter (Galatians 6:1) the whole church is urged to be actively involved in the process of restoration. The whole context breathes with deep compassion recognising that the best of us slip up. Indeed, the word Paul uses for 'someone caught in any kind of wrongdoing' does not mean deliberate, premeditated sin, but a slip that might happen to a man on an icy road or a dangerous path. It has a strong flavour of the unintentional. Paul is aware of the constant danger of those who are committed to walk with God being quick to judge the sins and failings of others with harshness. Paul is urging here that if anyone does slip then those who are spiritually mature should react by setting him right again and making sure that he is back on his feet. The word that he uses for 'to set right' or 'correct' is used for doing a repair so that what has been broken is mended and what has been functioning improperly can now function well. It is the word that is also used for a surgeon removing a growth from a man's body or in setting a limb which has been broken so that it will knit together again quickly. The whole tone of the instruction is centred not on punishment, but on cure. Restoration must always be carried out with the conscious attitude that I might well have been the one needing to be restored rather than being the one who is the instrument of restoration.

Any form of discipline then, whether it is a simple warning or the ultimate act of exclusion from functioning membership of the body of Christ, should always be understood as part of the total process of restoration. The goal of discipline is not exclusion, but restoration.

Maintaining purity

Honouring Christ by our obedience to his word and a concern to restore those who have failed and fallen are two important purposes of discipline. A third function of discipline is to maintain purity within the worshipping Christian community. In 1 Corinthians 5:6–8 the whole church is clearly seen to be affected by sin. In our own church some time ago someone had a picture (or was it a vision?) of a crowded room. In that crowd one or two were smoking. The tobacco smoke rose into the air and hung there. In a very short time everyone was affected by the smoke. All had inhaled some of it into their lungs, and everybody's clothes now carried it. The interpretation given was that when the congregation gathered there were frequently a few present who brought doubt and unbelief into the fellowship. Their attitude, reaction and contribution inevitably affected everyone present – it was automatic and undeniable. As a result we became concerned, when we met for worship, to restrain expressions of negatives and unbelief, and to encourage affirmation and faith-building. Sin, like smoke, permeates the whole body and so needs to be dealt with. The account of Achan's sin and the subsequent defeat of Joshua's army (Joshua 7) at Ai teaches clearly that purity is indispensable to power and that unchecked sin will cause weakness and ineffectiveness.

The presence of sin will often cause a very subtle 'feeling' that something is not right. This 'feeling' may not be general, but will be realised by those who are in responsible leadership within the fellowship. It will be sensed that somehow we have 'lost' something – without often being able to put a finger on it. Yet there will be an awareness that something of the sharp edge of spiritual excitement and expectancy has gone. The programme remains and we continue to go through the motions, but the spontaneous anticipation of what God is waiting and willing to do is now missing.

Fécamp Abbey is one of the most interesting ecclesiastical buildings in France. It was built in the twelfth century and has a spacious and impressive interior. Its magnificent memorials and tombs entice visitors from all over the world. Perhaps the chief charm of the abbey, however, is its glorious stained-glass windows. If they do not rival the stained-glass windows at Chartres, they are nevertheless among the most beautiful examples of the stainer's art. In 1928 the custodians of this old building gave instructions for the glass to be removed, restored, and cleaned. The expert who undertook this work completed the task but, just before the time came for putting the glass back, she was tempted by a large bribe to substitute an imitation and sell the abbey glass to America. She fell. The true glass crossed the Atlantic, a counterfeit was put in its place, and for six years the church was seen in a false light. Mysteriously the old glory had departed, and no one seemed to know why.

So it is with sin in a church fellowship. As in Fécamp Abbey, it was only when the deception was discovered, confessed, dealt with, and the stained-glass returned to its rightful place that the 'glory' of the building was restored. So sin needs to be identified, exposed, confessed and dealt with if power and relevance is to be experienced in the church. Only then can purity be maintained and power expected. The need for discipline is hard to swallow, but true.

The fourth purpose of discipline is to *discourage others* from sinning. As we have already seen (1 Timothy 5:20) the threat of publicity is no bad thing if it keeps a man in the right way, even from fear. It is true that to desire righteousness in order to please God and maintain our close walk with him is a much better motive for shunning all that we know is unacceptable to God, yet our hearts are not always motivated by godly desires and the fierce pressure can often strike us at unexpected times and in unlikely ways. Sometimes our fear of the consequences of sin is the best guardian of holiness.

So authority is invested in the church to exercise discipline. History records the ways in which this authority has been abused, and dishonour to the name of Christ has resulted. However, that authority to determine the extent of sin and act as heaven's representatives in dealing with it remains.

How awesome it is to take this teaching seriously and to follow these directives honourably! How well we need to know the heart of God and the guidance and enabling of his Holy Spirit! However, carelessness in the presence of sin is unacceptable and irresponsibility in ignoring it will bring its own dire and weakening consequences to the body of Christ on earth.

6

The joy-filled life

Some books are worth having on your bookshelf if only for their title. In 1970 I bought such a book by Basilea Schlinck – *Repentence: The Joy-filled Life*. Repentance can often be presented and understood as something which is dark and heavy and sombre. It was never intended to be so.

Is this joy really our (or my) experience? I often sense a heaviness among the people of God. I realise that there is a cross at the heart of the Christian faith, and that truly following Christ involves some rigorous self-denial – yet some of the most spiritual souls I have known have at the same time been the most joyful. Joy is not a weak word – it is not resignation wearing a wan smile. It is exuberant and, on occasions, boisterous. We are often so stiff with 'good manners' that we have even thought, in our inhibited way, that there is a touch of the vulgar in Christian joy! Yet one of the accompaniments of a new awareness and experience of the person and ministry of the Holy Spirit is a magnificent expression of Christian joy. Grimness and misery have been challenged and the flavour of joy has flowed as one of the expressions of the Spirit's fruit.

Hard-headed, down-to-earth men at the Feast of Pentecost long ago thought that the apostles were drunk, and whenever the pure living water of the Spirit of God has burst again from the rock, the same exuberant gladness, sooner or later, in one way or another, has broken forth. The early Franciscans had it – they were so happy they had to be reproved for laughing in church. The early Methodists had it and they stormed an unbelieving world with songs, some of them set to dance tunes (is there nothing new under the sun?). The early Salvationists had it. When Dr Farmer, the gifted and sophisticated organist at Harrow, pleaded with the Salvationist drummer not to hit the drum so hard, the beaming bandsman replied: 'Lor' bless you, Sir. Since I've been converted I'm so happy, I could bust the blooming drum!' (There certainly is nothing new under the sun!) All these expressions of joy were connected with the realisation of personal forgiveness, the consequence of repentance. Neither the early Franciscans, Methodists, nor Salvationists would mind that repentance implies we've done wrong, for the apostles would certainly have understood. With the reality of Pentecost in mind and the urgent questioning of the crowd, 'What shall we do?' they would recall the clear, unambiguous cry of the apostle Peter in response, 'Repent.'

Dr L P Jacks wrote a little book, *The Lost Radiance of the Christian Religion*. He said:

Christianity is the most encouraging, the most joyous, the least repressive, the least forbidding of all the religions of mankind. There is no religion which throws off the burden of life so completely, which escapes so swiftly from our moods, which gives so large a scope to the high spirits of the soul, and welcomes to its bosom with so warm an embrace those things of beauty which are joys forever . . . Christianity does not brood upon the sorrows of mankind. It is always music that you hear, and sometimes dancing as well.

The source of this joy is the grace (the sheer undeserved generosity of God) that assures forgiveness; and the key to that forgiveness, from our side, is repentance. Dr Jim Packer, in his book *I want to be a Christian*, affirms that when Peter, on the day of Pentecost, called the people to repent he 'was prescribing not a formal gesture of regret for the Crucifixion, but a total renunciation of independence as a way of living and a total submission to the rule of the risen Lord.' However unusual that may sound in our ears, that is the way to the joy-filled life. Dr A W Tozer in his book *Born after Midnight* says, 'Christ calls men to carry a cross; we call them to have fun in His Name. He calls them to forsake the world; we assure them, if they accept Jesus, the world will become their oyster. He calls them to suffer; we call them to enjoy all the bourgeois comforts modern civilisation affords. He calls them to holiness; we call them to a cheap and tawdry happiness.'

Here, as in so many other aspects of life, what we think is the way and what is in fact God's way are two entirely different things. 'Cheap grace', says Dietrich Bonhoeffer in his book *The Cost of Discipleship*, 'is the preaching of forgiveness without requiring repentance, baptism without church discipline, Communion without confession, absolution without personal confession. Cheap grace is grace without discipleship, grace without the Cross, grace without Jesus Christ, living and incarnate.'

Repentance revealed

Back in the early 1960s I was in the early years of an exciting and demanding ministry in Dunfermline. The 'honeymoon' period of a new ministry was over. I had taken the measure of the task to which I had been called and was somewhat alarmed at the size of it. I could see things that were wrong – and that is never too difficult, for there are always things that are wrong in a church. I spent the best part of a month working out how these things might be handled and dealt with. The more I worked on my formula for a new way forward the more excited I became. I could already see the breakthroughs that would surely come. I could already feel my pulse racing as I contemplated a new era. I had been long enough in ministry to realise that change did not come easily and difficult days would lie ahead. But this was my task and I was willing to accept the personal discomfort which would be involved. I had concluded that there were attitudes as well as activities which needed to be challenged and changed. It never occurred to me that there was a certain self-righteousness in all of this, since I saw the problem was clearly 'in them' rather than 'in me'.

Two friends of ours had invited Anne and me to supper in order to meet a friend of theirs from Bristol. I was unable to go in the early part of the evening since I had a deacons' meeting which, in fact, would be the one at which I could launch my programme for progress. Anne would have to go on her own and I would join them later when the deacons' meeting was over. It was all arranged and on the night we went our separate ways – I to the deacons and Anne for a social evening. Little did I know at that stage that it was not the deacons' meeting which was to change my future, but the supper encounter with an unknown visitor.

The deacons' meeting was friendly enough, but graciously they parried and turned down flat every proposal that I made. Frustration, disappointment and despair all mingled within me; what should I do? Resignation would not be all that difficult; although had I not felt strongly that God had called me here? For what purpose had God called me – to resign before this ministry had hardly begun?

In this frame of mind, the deacons' meeting over, I made my way, belatedly, to join the supper party. It was not a great distance from our church and the short walk was not sufficient for me to come to terms in my mind with what had happened earlier in the evening. I arrived to find the guest, a vicar from a large church in Bristol, in full flight, sharing his heart. He stopped long enough to greet me, but then picked up where he had left off. I wasn't in much of a mood to listen to another man's story. I was trying to put the broken pieces of my own story together. But now he was speaking about motivating and developing a large church. He was speaking about the criticism he had in his heart over a number of situations within the church. He was sharing how he had worked out a programme for progress and how his parochial church council had proved difficult to convince and unwilling to co-operate. He was talking about his personal frustration, disappointment and despair. He appeared not only to have been at the deacons' meeting I had just left, but he seemed to be right inside my own head and heart. I was listening now!

He spoke about how God had convicted him that the real problem did not lie 'out there' and 'with them', but 'in here' and 'with him'. He said he became aware of pride and pretentiousness in his own heart, and this quickly led to resentment and criticism of the way others were handling their responsibilities. 'Allow me to deal with your heart,' he said God was saying to him. 'Confess your own fault and repent of your own sin, and allow me the freedom to deal with my people instead of you,' God said.

It was a long night, and proved to be much longer after we left our friends' home. Anne and I spent a long time sharing our reactions to the evening – for both of us had been profoundly affected. I could not remember ever having been more clearly spoken to by God through one of his servants. That night we learned that we needed to call sin sin, and to begin to repent – not only of our bad works but also of our good works. I had to learn that anything that springs from self is sin. However small that might be it is still sin. Self-effort, or self-satisfaction in

77

service is sin. Self-pity in trials and difficulties; self-seeking, touchiness, resentment, and self-defence when I am hurt or injured by others; self-consciousness, reserve, worry, fear – all spring from self and all are sin, requiring confession, repentance and cleansing in the precious blood of Christ. My hard, unyielding self – which justifies itself, wants its own way, stands up for its rights and seeks its own glory – needs to bow to God's will (not in a fatalistic, mindless way, but in the glad and glorious acknowledgement that he is my Father, he loves me and has plans for me, and he will never let me down!). My self needs to admit its wrong, give up its own way to Jesus, surrender its rights, and discard its own glory – so that the Lord Jesus can live in me fully and reveal himself through me.

As I began to look at my Christian life I began to see how much of self there was (and is) in me. It dawned on me how much 'self' was trying to live the Christian life. The very fact that we use the word 'try' indicates that it is self that carries the responsibility. It is always self that gets irritable, envious, resentful, critical and worried. It is always self that becomes hard and unyielding in its attitudes to others. It is always self that is shy, self-conscious and reserved. As long as self is in control then God can do so little for us.

I began to realise that Jesus was willing to humble himself for me, and the only place where I could be motivated to live similarly was at his cross. Here is the one who is in the form of God, counting equality with God a thing not to be hung on to, but letting it go for us and becoming man, and not only man but servant man. There on the cross, as well as in his life, we see him willing to have no rights of his own, no home of his own, no possessions of his own; willing to let men revile him and yet never retaliate nor defend himself. Only the vision of the love that was willing to be broken for me can ever go on constraining me to be willing to learn to follow Christ.

Lord, bend that proud and stiffnecked I,
    Help me to bow the head and die;
Beholding Him on Calvary
    Who bowed His head for me.

As the weeks and months passed I began to realise that dying to self is not a thing we do once for all. It is forever a constant dying, for only then can the Lord Jesus be revealed constantly through us. All day long, and every day, the choice is before me in a thousand ways. I began to appreciate what I had long known intellectually; that the only life that pleases God is his life, and never ours, no matter how hard we try. It was slowly dawning on me how it was possible, even if extremely difficult, to live this way. We can never be filled with his life unless we are prepared for God to bring our life constantly to death. In this we need to co-operate by our moral choice.

George Muller, a Victorian to whom God gave thousands of orphans and more than a million pounds, was a man of God. Hard-pressed, on one occasion, to tell the secret of his spiritual life, George Muller said: 'There was a day when I died; utterly died,' and, as he spoke, he bent lower until he almost touched the floor. Continuing, he added: 'Died to George Muller, his opinions, preferences, tastes and will; died to the world, its approval or censure; died to the approval or blame even of my brethren and friends and, since then, I have studied only to show myself approved unto God.'

I owe so much to Roy Hession (author of *The Calvary Road*), Stanley Voke (author of *Reality*) and others in my learning about repentance. To enter in to what God has provided for me is not a matter of resolving to be humbler in the future. I needed to learn to repent of attitudes, reactions, words and deeds that are not acceptable to God. Our Lord Jesus did not become man, and slave/servant man at that, simply to give us an example, but that he might go to Calvary and die on the cross there for these very attitudes, reactions, words and deeds – so that on the basis of my confession and repentance these things might be cleansed away forever. The blood of Jesus, however, can never be applied to the sins of our proud hearts until we have repented of what has already happened and what we already are. This entails our willingness to allow the searching light of God the Holy Spirit to touch every part of our hearts and every part of our relationships. These very things which I accept, excuse, defend and rationalise are the very things which took Jesus to the cross. And on that cross he died that I might be forgiven and freed: he died to allow me to exchange my life for his.

As I entered further into fellowship with Christians who had been deeply affected by the East Africa Revival I began to realise the importance of repentance as the way to cleansing from sin, freedom from guilt and joy of heart. I also began to realise that repentance was a word which I knew well, but the content of which I had not fully appreciated nor the practice of which had I fully implemented. I gave myself to a lot of thought and study over repentance, and determined that whatever I discovered I would put into practice.

Repentance: the starting point

I became aware, as I searched the scriptures, that repentance was the main emphasis of the preaching of John the Baptist (Mark 1:4,5). Repentance was to be the means whereby the road would be prepared for our Lord Jesus to enter and do what God had given him to do. It seems that the four hundred years between the prophecy of Malachi (which marked the end of the Old Testament scriptures) and the gospel of Matthew (which marked the beginning of the New Testament scriptures) were marked by the silence of God. The first simple but unavoidable word that God had for his people after such a long silence was, 'Repent!' In this way a spiritual highway was being prepared for Jesus.

It is significant that a very few verses later on (Mark 1:14, 15) Jesus began his ministry on a similar note. The first area that needed to be tackled was not the political oppression and injustice of the Roman government; nor was it the empty, inconsistent, insensitive legalism of Pharisaical Judaism; nor was it the dark, sinister encroachment of the demonic powers of darkness – it was the sinfulness of the human heart. Jesus declared that 'the Kingdom of God is near!' (ie the government or rule of God is near!) and that the way to begin to live in the freedom, joy and authority of that kingdom was to learn how to repent.

So it was, also, on the Day of Pentecost. Having known the purging of fire and the power of the 'rushing mighty wind' praise gave way to preaching and the insistent note of that preaching was 'for God's sake and for your own sakes, repent!' (Acts 2:37–39).

In all of this I saw clearly that the transformation of religion into reality lay in repentance. I also began to realise that Calvary preceded Pentecost not simply in history, but also in my experience – there could be no Pentecostal power without Calvary pain. I recognised that Jesus surely did not come to destroy me, but to redeem me – but that the surgeon often has to cut deeply into our flesh to rid us of the things which cripple, destroy, and prevent healthy growth. Cleansing and forgiveness are mandatory for spiritual development and spiritual health.

I became convinced that the devil did two things with sin. He either minimised it or he magnified it. He was unconcerned whether I became insensitive to sin or introspective over it; either way I would be trapped into living with it. I could easily be persuaded that 'it is natural to be/feel like that!' and 'everyone is like that, Jim!' The result would be to settle for putting up with attitudes, behaviour, reactions and so on that are quite unacceptable to God. I am not an introspective person, but I could see others who were, and they would constantly be searching around for some sin or another as they daily recognised their unworthiness. The devil rubs his hands with satisfaction whether he drives us to one extreme or the other.

It was, however, with equal conviction that I rejoiced in a new way that God also does two things with sin – he deals with it and then he dismisses it. 1 John 1:7 became a focal point for me: 'But if we live in the light – just as he is in the light – then we have fellowship with one another, and the blood of Jesus, his Son, purifies us [or "goes on cleansing us"] from every sin.' That whole first chapter of John's first letter burned with a new brightness in my understanding. What more could I, or anyone else, ever ask than that unambiguous promise of 1 John 1:9: 'But if we confess our sins to God, he will keep his promise and do what is right: he will forgive us our sins and purify us from all our wrongdoing.'

To believe that the blood of Jesus, God's son, 'goes on' cleansing from all sin without exception is part of the good news we have to declare. So God deals with sin in an absolute way – and then he dismisses it. He puts it behind his back (where he can no longer see it or be reminded of it!); he buries it in the depths of the sea (because it is dead and gone!); he does not ever remember it again (it is not only out of sight, but also out of mind!); he removes it from us as far as the east is from the west (and that is infinity!). No wonder the scholarly and godly John Duncan, Professor of Semitic Languages at New College in Edinburgh (often affectionately referred to as Rabbi Duncan!) was seen in his old age walking down Edinburgh's Princes Street with what seemed to be a skip in his step, if not a dance. A friend met him and stopped his progress for a moment. 'Dr Duncan,' he said, 'you must have heard some good news today!' 'News?' exclaimed John Duncan, 'News? The best of all news: "The blood of Jesus, God's Son, goes on cleansing us from all sin." '

So it was that I realised that I will never be a faultless man, but I am a forgiven man; perfection will forever elude me in this life, but pardon is my birth-right in

God. Failure may be my companion again and again, but forgiveness is offered to me, and not condemnation. This does not encourage irresponsibility or carelessness, but rather wonder, gratitude and love, and the determination that, God helping me, I will not fall or fail at that point again. The devil's desire is to keep me under condemnation because of the weakness of my humanity, but the Spirit's desire is to convict me so that I will be quickly led to repentance, confession, forgiveness and freedom to become all that God always intended me to be. Repentance is so strategic to it all – so that I can enter into all that God has provided.

Steps to repentance

How do I repent? There are five elements in repentance. First of all I need to come to a *knowledge of sin*. I need to recognise what sin is and call it by its name without excusing it or justifying it. There are five main words for sin in the New Testament. When taken together and properly understood they give a full understanding of what sin is.

The first of these words is *hamartia*. This is basically a shooting term and means to miss the mark or the target. Sin is just that. There is a standard (or a target) of excellence which God has clearly defined and to which our conscience readily responds. As I set my life against that standard I become aware that I am not what I ought to be – and in my heart of hearts I am not what I long to be. Fear often takes the place of faith; cynicism sometimes destroys trust; isolation, from time to time, is desired more than fellowship; disobedience appears more acceptable and sometimes more reasonable than obedience; unbelief would often seem to fit the facts of the matter more than belief; attitudes, reactions, prejudices, personal preferences are all areas that leave me aware of fault and failure. From time to time I have been aware that I have approached God not on the basis of his grace, but on the basis of my good works. I have seen how subtle this can be, but how dangerous in undermining the foundations of the gospel. Bad works need never keep us out of heaven, but good works will surely never get us in. All of this and so much more is unacceptable to God; it is not the standard he has set; it is sin.

I need to be definite and clear about this. In what areas of my life do these things occur and how? Is it in the area of my personal life, my marriage, my family life, my work, my church life? Where? When? How do these things occur?

The second word for sin in the New Testament is *parabasis*. This has within it the idea of something which is deliberate and premeditated. It operates in the area of my choice, my will, my knowledge. This kind of sinning occurs when I find myself saying or thinking: 'I know I should not be doing this/saying this/feeling this', but going straight ahead to do it, say it or and nourish my wrong feelings. Parabasis is a word which means 'to step across'. This refers to assessing the situation and then making a judgment (in this case a wrong judgment) on which action is then taken. However reasonable and natural we may convince ourselves our action is, if it is not acceptable to God, then it is wrong and so is sin. How easy it is to justify wrong things! How corrosive this is to our walk with God and our effectiveness in his service. The way of God is always that we would recognise sin for what it is and repent of it.

The third word for sin in the New Testament is *paraptōma* and it is the opposite of parabasis. Paraptōma has a flavour of the unpremeditated – it is impulsive, unintentional sin. It occurs when I am caught off-guard for a variety of reasons. Paraptōma really means 'to slip across'. When I am in conversation with someone and I say something wrong which I never intended to say – that is paraptōma. How often we catch ourselves saying or thinking, 'I don't know why I said that, it just slipped out' – that is paraptōma. Sometimes we do something for which we are afterwards sorry and on reflection we cannot imagine why it was we did it – that is paraptōma. However unscheduled and unintentional, it is still sin, and needs to be recognised and dealt with.

The fourth word for sin the New Testament is *anomia*. This describes the basic human instinct to do what *I* want to do, as and when and where I like. I am aware that I should not, it is forbidden; but I am my own man and I do not care who says no or is displeased, I will still do it. It is best translated 'lawlessness'. Anomia occurs when I take the law into my own hands and become a law unto myself. This is so contrary to living within the family of God and recognising God's love and grace towards me.

When Queen Elizabeth II was a tiny girl, and still Princess Elizabeth, she was caught by her grandfather – the late King George V – doing something which was forbidden. He checked her and then chastised her. She apparently stamped her foot in a tantrum and said, 'I am a princess, and I will do what I like.' To this the wise old grandfather replied, 'My dear, you are a princess, and because of that you will never be able to do what you like.'

So it is in the family of God. I am set free because of what Jesus has done for me – but I am not free to do what I like, but free to do what he likes. This, of course, is true freedom. God always knows what is best for me, even when it conflicts with my plans and preferences. Lawlessness is sin – indeed it was the first sin which manifested itself in the garden of Eden.

The final word for sin in the New Testament is *opheilēma*. It means my failure to pay what is my due and responsibility to either man or God (or both). I think few of us would ever make the claim that we have always fulfilled our obligation to both man and God. Often opheilēma is translated 'debt' – and it ought to be so translated in the Lord's Prayer (rather than 'trespass'). Such 'debts' need to be forgiven, and our part is to recognise the areas where we have failed and repent of them.

So we need to come to a knowledge of sin if we are going to repent properly. We need to recognise what sin is in a biblical sense and refuse to call it by any other name.

Step two
The second element in repentance is *sorrow*. I need to feel sorry for the sin which I have just identified. It is not enough to be clinically honest in recognising sin, but I need to feel as God feels about it and see it from his point of view. We often can be so calm and unmoved by the things which literally tore the beloved Son of God apart. Although this has a strong emotional content it has a very firm spiritual base.

Feelings of sorrow, like most feelings, cannot be switched on and off at will. It will help to meditate upon passages in the Bible which record God's love and Jesus' death, and to begin to see what my sin does and has done. This is facing objective reality. Often to dwell on the realities portrayed in the communion service will help us respond to sin with sorrow. Some of the great hymns which are used at communion or Easter – hymns which speak of the passion of Christ – will cause our sorrow to be real and will give the Holy Spirit the opportunity to do his work in this way. Why not listen to these hymns on tape rather than simply read their words in a book?

Such sorrow is not a superficial emotional spasm, but the willing acceptance of the ministry of the Holy Spirit. He wants to touch our hearts as well as our heads. He wants to stimulate our feelings as well as our understanding and our will.

Step three
The third element in repentance has to do with our lips and voice. We need to *confess* the sin which we have isolated and sorrowed over. The only way that sin leaves the body is through the mouth. There is a spiritual dynamic in confession which I find difficult to understand and even more difficult to express. All I do know is that

something happens when I am prepared to confess my faith or to confess my failure. Confessing my faith has an incredible effect in stabilising and strengthening me and giving a new solidity to that which I confess. Confessing my fault is part of the dynamic process of setting me free in order to become what God wants me to be.

I do not think it is always possible, nor is it always necessary, to confess sin to someone else (although there is a far greater richness and reality in that than I was brought up to believe!). But to verbalise in specific detail what it is I am concerned to get clear of, with or without someone present, has a remarkable effect. I have also found that to write it down on a piece of paper and present it to the Lord for cleansing can have an equally freeing effect.

God cannot deal with something which we want to excuse, justify or accept. My verbal or written confession is a declaration that I believe this thing, whether attitude or activity, is wrong and I want to be free of it. My confession is an indication that I really agree with God about that thing.

Step four
The fourth element in repentance is *turning away* from that sin. Part of repentance involves being sorry enough about what I am confessing to stop doing it! So much of the Christian life is lived in the area of the will. On the cross Jesus died so that I could be freed and forgiven. The Holy Spirit has come to enable me to live in the reality of the freedom and forgiveness that Jesus has made possible. Jesus came not only to forgive our sin but to set us free to live in righteousness. 'No one born (begotten) of God,' cries John, '[deliberately and knowingly] habitually practises sin, for God's nature abides in him – His principle of life, the divine sperm remains permanently within him – and he cannot practise sinning because he is born (begotten) of God' (1 John 3:9 Amplified Bible). No one who is really born of God can go on and on committing

sin and ignore the need to do something about it. The
habitual life of a child of God is to do right – although
occasionally he will do wrong. When he is aware, however, that he is doing wrong, he will repent of it and
determine to walk in God's way of righteousness. Christians may fall into sin, but they are unable to live in it
once they are aware of it. So our wills are involved in
repentance as well as our mouths and our minds and our
hearts.

The Holy Spirit has freed us to do right. There is no
easy road to this. It requires the discipline and determination of our wills. The moment, however, we choose to
do right then the Holy Spirit comes alongside us to help
us to do just that – this is part of the thrilling good news
of God.

Step five

The fifth part of repentance is not always possible and,
indeed, is not always appropriate. How wise and sensitive
we need to be here! Whenever it is possible and appropriate, however, we need to *make restitution* for the sin that
has been identified. A few years ago, at Spring Harvest,
I met a young man whom I did not immediately recognise.
After a very few minutes I did remember. He came to
our church some years ago. Then he was a raw, abrasive,
likeable cockney. Life had been difficult for him and he
had been released from prison. Some folks within our
fellowship loved, cared for and encouraged him. It was
not at all difficult because of what could only be described
as his lovely personality; but to bring discipline and order
into his life was difficult to the point of total impossibility.
He came to Christ and acknowledged him as his Lord
and saviour, and that was wonderful and real. The same
ebullient, apparently ungovernable nature continued.
Eventually he left us to go north and I lost touch with
him. He had gone and I really had forgotten him. Now,
years afterward, he came up to me at Spring Harvest and
we were re-united – and I was introduced to his wife and

family. What a change! Now a mature, responsible gifted man stood before me. He gave me £20. Apparently when he had been with us at Gold Hill, years before, he had stolen goods from our bookshop, valued at £15. I can remember there was some talk about thefts from the bookshop, but that was so long ago and no one was ever identified for having been responsible. Now after ten years or more he was giving me £20 and was asking that the extra £5 should cover the interest on the original £15. He was also asking forgiveness for his sin. This is restitution. He was free from something in his past for which God had forgiven him, but there was still something to put right with those he had wronged. He was able to do this with great grace.

I met him only a few months ago, and I understand that he is now a leader in his local church and from time to time ministers the word of God. Without doubt there was joy – not simply the joy of a bright, optimistic, resilient temperament, but the joy of a man living in a simple, uncomplicated relationship with God, having put things right with others.

The way of joy

In a churchyard in Olney, in the heart of England, lie the remains of a man whose influence has been felt throughout the world. John Newton came into a church which was in the grip of the political bishop, the fox-hunting parson, and an utterly worldly and materialistic laity. In his *History of the Church of England*, Wakeman gives us this sordid and terrible picture of the church as Newton found it. John Newton and a few kindred spirits were the 'first generation of the clergy called "evangelical" and they were to become – to use Sir James Stephens' famous phrase – "the second founders of the Church of England".' Newton became one of the founders of the Church Missionary Society and through that, as well as through the lives of those that he influenced who went on to have nation-wide and international impact, he influenced the whole world.

John Newton wrote his own epitaph, and it stands in Olney to this day:

JOHN NEWTON
Clerk,
Once an Infidel and Libertine,
A Servant of Slaves in Africa
was
By the Mercy of our Lord and Saviour
Jesus Christ,
Preserved, Restored, Pardoned,
And Appointed to Preach the Faith he
had so long laboured to destroy.

He himself tells, 'I was born in a home of godliness, and dedicated to God in my infancy. I was my mother's only child, and almost her whole employment was the care of my education.' Every day of her life she prayed with him, as well as for him, and every day she was concerned to store his mind with scripture so that he could memorise it and allow it to affect his life. Although John Newton's mother died when he was seven years old, she had laid a good foundation.

Having lost his mother at seven – the one certainty and stability in his early life – he went to sea when he was eleven years old. The years passed and he tells us that he eventually went to Africa 'that I might be free to sin to my heart's content.' During the next years his soul was assaulted by the most horrendous experiences. He endured the awesome barbarities of life before the mast; he fell into the pitiless clutches of a press gang; as a deserter from the navy he was flogged until the blood streamed down his back; and he became involved in the unbelievable atrocities of the African slave trade. Going from bad to worse he actually became a slave himself! The slave of a slave! He was sold to an African woman who, glorifying in her power over him, made him depend for his food on the crusts that she tossed under her table! His abject degradation was complete. In later years he could never recall some of these experiences without a shudder. As he says in his self-composed epitaph he was 'the servant of slaves.'

On the tenth of March, 1748, in the midst of a terrifying storm at sea when his ship was plunging down into the troughs and the hold was rapidly filling with water and few on board expected to survive, Newton was hurrying to the pumps as ordered. He said to the ship's captain, 'If this will not do, the Lord have mercy upon us!' His own words actually startled him. 'Mercy!' he said to himself in blank astonishment, 'Mercy! Mercy! What mercy can there be for me? This was the first desire I had breathed for mercy for many years! About six in the evening the hold was free from water, and then came a gleam of hope. I thought I saw the hand of God displayed in our favour. I began to pray. I could not utter the prayer of faith. I could not draw near to a reconciled God and call Him Father. My prayer for mercy was like the cry of the ravens, which yet the Lord Jesus does not disdain to hear. In the gospel I saw at least a peradventure of hope; but on every other side I was surrounded with black, unfathomable despair.'

At the age of 23 John Newton reached out to God in penitence and faith and God heard him and met him. Later he was to say, 'That tenth of March is a day much to be remembered by me; I have never suffered it to pass unnoticed since the year 1748. For on that day – March 10, 1748 – the Lord came from on high and delivered me out of deep waters.' So it was that repentance led to reality and that reality included freedom, joy and gratitude. Hymns began to flow from Newton's heart – 'How sweet the Name of Jesus sounds', 'Glorious things of Thee are spoken, Zion, City of our God', 'One there is above all others', and perhaps the best known and most greatly loved of them all, 'Amazing grace, how sweet the sound that saved a wretch like me'. All of these express the reality of joy and wonder which must always be the accompaniment of repentance. Repentance not only brings us out of captivity, but also brings us into freedom.

When John Newton's powers were fast failing, and he was becoming very frail and aware that through the years his memory had often betrayed him, he said, 'My memory is nearly gone; but I remember two things, that I am a great sinner and that Christ is a great Saviour!' This is the recipe for a joy-filled life.

7

'Take it . . . it was meant for you'

Long ago in Edinburgh's New College Professor John Duncan created an unforgettable impact. Whatever might be said about this scholarly, godly man, he could never be ignored. There are many stories that are told, and retold, about him. I would imagine that most of them are true. One of the most famous of these stories is told about him when once he was serving communion. He noticed a woman hesitating to take the cup, and so he said to her gently: 'Take it, woman. It was meant for sinners. It was meant for you.' In this act of communion we are not just dwelling in the distant realms of memory; we recall a historical reality and we receive afresh and enter into what has been done for us in our Lord Jesus Christ.

A sacrament of memory

It is easy to forget. If I were asked what causes more damage – things remembered which should have been forgotten, or things forgotten which should have been remembered, I would say the former without doubt. Yet forgetfulness can be such an impoverishing thing. Our Lord Jesus quite clearly recognised this when he instituted the Lord's Supper. This sacrament is the sacrament of memory. The central instruction for the Lord's Supper is: 'Do this in memory of me' (1 Corinthians 11:24). This is the heart of the whole matter. To some this will seem strange, while others feel that this view of the Lord's Supper is inadequate.

How is this 'sacrament of memory' strange? Because normally when we want to remember someone we want to think of them in life rather than in the wan, emaciated, tense humiliation of death. My mother died of cancer in the Western Infirmary in Glasgow. Her flesh had been devoured, her bones had crumbled, her hormones had been cruelly disorientated. She was, after two years, hardly recognisable except to those of us who loved her dearly. We do not have photographs of that devastation – only fading and painful memories that go back, now, more than thirty years. We do have photographs of her silver wedding celebrations with my father. She was a pretty and generous woman. That is how I remember her – and that I think is how she would want it to be. But not so Jesus. He wanted us to recall the torn flesh, the bleeding wounds, the gaunt cross, the loneliness, shame and humiliation of it. 'This is my body, broken . . . This is my blood, shed . . . Remember me this way,' he said.

Others feel that the sacrament of memory is more than just that. However we need to think clearly about what memory is. It is impossible to *only* remember. Memory brings companions with it. We always remember for some purpose or to some effect. Our memories never operate in a vacuum. What then is the purpose and the effect of this sacramental memory? It is simplistic and misleading to speak of the Lord's Supper as 'a mere memorial'.

Remember what Christ has done
In our remembering we realise with awe what our Lord Jesus Christ has done and suffered for us. It is so easy to lose the cutting-edge of emotion and realisation. It is possible to share the supper and still remain unmoved.

The tradition in which I was raised encouraged such an arid and often empty formality. We celebrated the Lord's Supper at the end of every Sunday morning service. That was all right in itself, but it was 'tacked on' as an addendum to what had gone before. It was the tail-piece rather than the central act and climax of our worship. It always seemed to me to be an optional extra for the worshipping community rather than the eagerly awaited opportunity for obedience. I am convinced, however, that it was the form, the structure, the timing, the attitude that was wrong rather than the reality itself. The Lord's Supper can and should be a vivid picture; a powerful encounter with the reality of what Jesus Christ did and suffered for me. It is there that love and gratitude and wonder are rekindled and devotion is reborn.

As I remember that it was for *me* that he died, then I can begin to grasp with fresh joy the benefits. 'This is my body, which is *for you*,' he said. We need to receive again and again because we sin again and again and need forgiveness again and again. In our Wednesday morning communion service, when the participants come forward to receive the bread and wine, I have often been deeply moved as hands are stretched out – work-worn, well-lived-in hands, yet like the extended, open hands of little children open to receive. I cannot always see the faces of those who come with outstretched hands because the head is bowed in penitence, humility and worship, but I sometimes see the tears – of sorrow for sin, of gratitude for grace – that trickle down and drop silently onto the communion rail and the carpet. Emotion? Yes, surely that: but more than that – reality! What a wonder! What a privilege! How humbling it is for me to be allowed to serve in the simplicity of the Lord's Supper and to say with heartfelt encouragement (using words from the Anglican liturgy), 'Feed on him (Christ) in your hearts by faith with thanksgiving,' and to say with conviction, 'The blood of Jesus goes on cleansing from all sin.' We are remembering something done for us so that we may receive it for ourselves once again.

However, in the Lord's Supper there is more than a memory of a reality to be received once more. We are not remembering someone who is dead and gone forever. That is the paralysing experience of bereavement – he was here, but now he is gone forever! But in communion we are not remembering someone who took his place in the pages of a history book and who must now forever be in the past. We are remembering someone who not only was cruelly beaten and crucified, pronounced dead and buried; but who was dramatically, unexpectedly, but unmistakably raised to life again. We are remembering someone who died, but is now alive! In the sacrament we have more than a memory; we encounter the risen Christ.

Remember that Christ is present
In spite of the formality and emptiness of the communion services of the tradition in which I was raised, the one persisting fragrant experience from those days was the use of a communion hymn during those services. I loved (and still do!) these hymns, for they set up deep longings in my heart and lifted my anticipation that there was more (much more!) than what I was then experiencing. One of these powerful hymns was 'Here, O my Lord, I see Thee face to face.' Really? Yes, really! Even to this day not only do the words stir me, but so does the tune we used to sing it to. So much is this so that a variety of organists with whom I have worked through the years have become amused at my clumsy attempts to use that tune to as many hymns as have the same musical metre. But the words remain hauntingly relevant to me in my beleaguered humanity and frailty:

Here, O my Lord, I see Thee face to face;
Here would I touch and handle things unseen,
Here grasp with firmer hand the eternal grace,
And all my weariness upon Thee lean.

This is the hour of banquet and of song;

This is the heavenly table spread for me:
Here let me feast, and, feasting, still prolong
The brief, bright hour of fellowship with Thee.

Nineteenth-century language, but Horatius Bonar expresses how the real presence of Jesus Christ in the sacrament is remembered. The risen Lord is universally present. He is not present in the sacrament any more than he is present anywhere else. Brother Lawrence long ago said he felt as near to the Lord when he was washing the greasy dishes in the monastery kitchen as he ever did at the blessed sacrament. For him that may well have been true, but for many of us the sacrament of the Lord's Supper is the place at which we become aware of that presence. It is not so much that he is specially present as it is that we are made aware of his presence. The Lord's Supper then is encounter with the risen Christ.

'A mere memorial', then, is a very misleading phrase. Memory normally has a purpose, and, even if it has no purpose, it certainly has an effect. The effect of my remembering is to realise exactly what has happened historically and that it was for me. To realise what Jesus Christ did, is to be moved to take as my own – to receive – what was done on my behalf. Such receiving leads me once more to an encounter with a living Lord, risen and reigning.

The implication of all of this for forgiveness and for forgiving is beyond measure. It is indispensable.

Remember our commitment
All of this remembering must end in another act on our part – it must end in renewed commitment, availability and dedication. This is to recapture the other meaning of the word *sacramentum* (the Latin word from which we get our word sacrament). The sacramentum was the soldier's oath of loyalty to his commanding officer or the citizen's vow to his emperor. King Arthur is alleged to have said of his now legendary knights,

I made them lay their hands in mine
And swear to reverence the King.

Napoleon Bonaparte had a number of picked soldiers
whom he called 'The Old Guard'. He knew he could trust
them through thick and thin, and in the many anxious
moments that Napoleon passed through he was comforted
when he could turn to his Old Guard. They stood by him;
they were loyal to the core; they never wavered in their
commitment to their emperor and commander. One day,
however, it was whispered that there was a rebellion in
the Old Guard. This stung Napoleon deeply. Was it true?
If so, what would he do? He summoned the entire Old
Guard to the Palace Court. They waited outside in the
courtyard, while Napoleon sat alone in the throne room.

The Old Guard wondered what would happen. Censure? dismissal? cashiered? punishment? imprisonment?
worse? What had the chief in mind? A messenger came
out and summoned the members of the Old Guard one
by one into the presence of Napoleon. The first man came
in at the far door. The door was closed, and he was alone
with the Emperor. He walked right up to the throne until
he stood face to face with Napoleon, and not a word was
spoken. Napoleon looked into his eyes and he looked
into the eyes of his chief, and then Napoleon stretched
out his hand and they gripped hands – and the guardsman
left by the rear door. And the next man came in, and
never a word was spoken. He walked up to the throne,
stood, and looked; again the hand-shake, and he moved
out of the throne room. The next man came – the same
look, the same out-stretched hand – and the next. The
rebellion was over forever.

So it is in the sacrament. In the receiving of the bread
and wine, as it were from the very hands of Jesus himself,
there is that brief, yet holy, personal divine encounter.
We are able to come with all our failure, shame and folly,
with all our mingling motives and emotions, and to see
his tenderness and righteousness, to see the understanding

and love in his eyes and to touch the depths of his heart. We can know the unspoken communication between us of, 'I am so sorry that I have sinned against you and against others. I now repent and ask for your forgiveness for all that is past,' and to know that he says, 'Child, I forgive you, go and sin no more.' The security of being forgiven allows us to add one more thing: to say, 'I will serve you from this day forward to the glory of your name.'

Who can understand the richness of his mercy and the infinity of his grace? I can never earn his favour, but I can receive it. How can I honestly and honourably receive without demonstrating the reality of my gratitude by putting myself entirely at his disposal? This is the sacrament.

When Marshal Foch took over the supreme command of the Allied armies in France and Flanders during World War I, General Pershing said to him, 'Here we are, Foch: all that we have and are; dispose of us as you will.' To our commander, our chief, we cannot do other than that as we come to the communion service.

A dramatic sign

T C Edwards, in his commentary on 1 Corinthians, simply says, 'The Lord's Supper is the unchanging statement of that which is unchanging in Christianity. The centre of Christianity is what Jesus did. The Lord's Supper in its dramatic picture states that just as it is. Preaching talks about it; theology interprets it and conceptualises it. The sacrament announces it. The Lord's Supper is the permanent dramatic pronouncement of the unchanging divine action in Jesus Christ, which theology interprets and reinterprets continuously.'

Here is something which is vital to forgiveness. The sacrament not only affirms the reality that I am forgiven, but gives me the security to release in forgiveness those who have wronged me. Many of us struggle with feelings of shame and sinfulness, and we are so prone to hold on to the hurts that we have received at the hands of others. We have found it an enormous release to receive forgiveness and to give forgiveness as we have reached out in faith to receive broken bread and out-poured wine. Over the years as I have observed thousands 'feeding on Christ by faith with thanksgiving in their hearts' I am persuaded that this is so. The Lord's Supper is not so much preaching (although in the widest and most significant sense it is that – powerful and eloquent) as it is participation in a dramatic sign.

Looking up

In communion we look *up* – with gratitude. For centuries the gathered church has been declaring the reality which is proclaimed by a well-known contemporary worship song:

> As we are gathered, Jesus is here;
> one with each other, Jesus is here;
> joined by the Spirit, washed in the blood,
> part of the body, the church of God.

So it is in communion. The mystery is that we not only feed *on* Christ, we feed *with* Christ.

Looking back

In Communion we look *back* – with wonder. 'Remember me this way!' urges Jesus. 'Remember me with my body beaten, broken, bleeding, dying.' As I look back what do I see? I see God become man; the divine become human. But I also see the eternal dying. How can it be that the immortal dies? As I look back I realise that while salvation is free it is never cheap. God who is spirit becomes flesh. God – eternal and immortal – is incarnate and dies! The only real response to a clear understanding of this is wonder. This is what it took to secure my forgiveness! This is what it cost to set me free!

Looking within

In communion we look *within* – with honesty and without fear of unhealthy introspection. The apostle Paul gives clear, practical guidelines for those who would look for reality in the Lord's Supper. 'So then,' he says, 'everyone should examine himself first, and then eat the bread and drink from the cup.'

At the very end of the hymn book that is used by the denomination within which I work are a number of hymns which are designated 'Mainly for Private Use'. I don't know how many would take advantage of this section. There are two hymns there, however, which I have used 'privately' from time to time. One of these begins,

Show me myself, O holy Lord;
    Help me to look within;
I will not turn me from the sight
    Of all my sin.

It continues in its nineteenth-century way:

Just as it is in Thy pure eyes
    Would I behold my heart;
Bring every hidden spot to light,
    Nor shrink the smart.

This is meaningful to me – if not to everyone! Christianity allows me to be real about the world around me – with all its pain and want, frustration and heartbreak. It also allows me to be real about the God above me – because it proclaims that God has taken the initiative and has revealed himself to man. But Christianity also allows me to be real about myself – I am a man who is pardoned, but not perfect; I am a man who is forgiven, but not faultless. This is not to excuse or overlook my weaknesses and imperfections, but it does allow me to confront them in a realistic and practical way – and the focal point for all of this is the Lord's Supper. This does not lead me to crushing despair, but to boundless hope because the blood of Jesus Christ, God's Son, cleanses (and goes on cleansing) me from all sin. In the sacrament I am reminded that God not only deals with my sin, but he dismisses it perfectly for ever – it is now out of his sight and out of his mind. In repentance and faith (and in the physical act of receiving bread and wine) I stand before God as someone who has never sinned in any way or to any degree ever before.

Sometimes, however, it's still hard not to feel guilty, even after forgiveness has been portrayed and experienced in such a powerful way. We want to be like Christian in Bunyan's *Pilgrim's Progress*, who is shown as bringing a great burden to the cross, at the sight of which the ropes which bind the burden to him are broken and the burden rolls downhill and out of sight. Sometimes it is helpful to share the progress of forgiveness with another person. This involves sharing the detail of what has been forgiven. However awkward and embarrassing this might be it does help us feel we've got rid of the matter which made us feel so guilty.

Another practical means of grasping our forgiveness is to note down on a piece of paper the matters which we have confessed and which God has forgiven. Then write 1 Peter 5:7, 'Leave all your worries with him, because he cares for you,' in bold letters across it all. Consciously hand over each matter to God – and then tear up or burn the piece of paper, watching the burdensome, guilt-making past disappear.

Yet another possibility is to adopt Richard Foster's helpful meditation exercise from *Celebration of Discipline* (Hodder and Stoughton). 'Begin', he says, 'by placing your palms down as a symbolic indication of your desire to turn over any concerns you may have to God. . . . Whatever it is that weighs on your mind or is a concern to you, just say, "palms down." Release it. You may even feel a certain sense of release in your hands. After several moments of surrender, turn your palms up as a symbol of your desire to receive from the Lord. Perhaps you will pray silently . . . whatever you need, you say, "palms up." Having centred down, spend the remaining moments in complete silence. Do not ask for anything. Allow the Lord to commune with your spirit, to love you. If impressions or directions come, fine; if not, fine.'

What a wonder it is to believe and receive the forgiveness which God offers us! So it should be no surprise that frequently our communion services conclude in unhindered joy and exuberant praise and thanksgiving. Such is the relief that comes through the realisation that the perfect sacrifice of Jesus has enabled *me* to be forgiven.

Looking around

In Communion we look *around* – with love. Communion is not a 'love feast'. Historically the 'love feast' or the fellowship meal preceded the Lord's Supper. And yet in communion we are expressing not only a strong and unhindered relationship with our heavenly Father, but also with our brothers and sisters. The cross of Christ broke down the barriers, created by sin, between God and man; but also it removed the barriers between people. It is not possible to have one without the other. To be out of fellowship with another Christian is automatically to be out of fellowship with my Father God. In the same way, to be out of fellowship with my Father God will lead to my being out of fellowship with other Christians. We become related to Christ singly, but we cannot live in him separately. There is no such thing in the Bible as solitary religion. Religion may well be a personal affair, but it can never be private. Spiritual reality cannot be measured by a vague feeling of oneness with God, but by the state of my relationships with others within God's family.

What upset the apostle Paul so much as he wrote to the Christians in Corinth (1 Corinthians 11:17–22), was that they were behaving in a selfish, proud and inconsiderate way. They lacked sensitivity towards one another. Paul verbally thrashes them for dishonouring the Lord's table by their attitudes towards one another.

My own understanding of the communion service has been immeasurably enriched by the practice of the Anglican Church. My Free Church instincts were critical of anything written and liturgical. I had been schooled to believe that such practices led to a sterile formality. Liturgical worship automatically spelt loss of spiritual liberty. Of course it can, but so-called 'free' forms of worship can be as empty and arid and every bit as formal as the most formal written liturgy. Then I experienced the Anglican communion service. I was moved, impressed and helped by the progression of the service, the simplicity and beauty of the prayers, the honour that was given to the word of God, the dignity with which the elements of bread and wine were handled and dispensed, the authority of the words of absolution, and the tender, gentle sharing of the peace.

The sharing of the peace impressed me most when I was at a conference at Ashburnham Place in Sussex. I had never been allowed to move around in communion before – far less greet those around me and bless them with the peace of Christ. (It was much later that I came to realise that the peace gave an opportunity to put things right with anyone where coldness or criticism was spoiling our relationship.) So it was that it was possible to come to that high moment of receiving the bread and the wine unhindered by any shadows caused through a break in fellowship. The peace gave the opportunity to look *around* with love.

Looking forward

Finally, in communion, we look *forward* – with confidence and expectation. The Lord's Supper is to be observed only 'until he comes'. It is a reminder that we are living between the two great events in human history – the first and the second comings of our Lord Jesus Christ. Christ has already come – and we celebrate that at Christmas time. But for every mention in the Bible that Jesus would come and came on that first Christmas morning, there are eight mentions of the second coming of Christ – not in the weakness of a little child, but in the strength and splendour of the Lord of glory. One verse in thirty refers to this 'divine far-off event to which the whole of creation is moving.' Of the twenty-seven New Testament books and letters twenty-three refer to it. Some devote most of their content to it, whilst others devote whole chapters to it. It is mentioned more than twelve hundred times in the Old Testament, and more than three hundred in the New Testament.

John confidently affirms, 'See how much the Father has loved us! His love is so great that we are called God's children – and so, in fact, we are. This is why the world does not know us: it has not known God. My dear friends, we are now God's children, but it is not yet clear what we shall become. But we know that when Christ appears, we shall be like him, because we shall see him as he really is. Everyone who has this hope in Christ keeps himself pure, just as Christ is pure' (1 John 3:1–3).

So in the Lord's Supper I – in fellowship with others – look *up*, with gratitude; look *back*, with wonder; look *within*, with honesty; look *around*, with love; and look *forward*, with confidence and expectation. It is not possible to be involved in such an experience without being deeply affected and, in fact, transformed. So the Lord's Supper was ever intended to be. It is provided to minister the sheer undeserved generosity of the heart of God to us.

Communion is important!

Augustine, the fifth-century Bishop of Hippo in north Africa once said: 'Our Lord Jesus Christ hath knit together a company of new people by sacraments, most few in number, most easy to be kept, most excellent in signification.' The sacraments of baptism and the Lord's Supper are the 'effectual (which means they can *do* something, they're powerful) signs of grace' that were instituted by our Lord Jesus Christ. They are the outward and visible signs of the blessings of the gospel that are given by God and received by faith. They are a constant reminder of the dynamic love of God taking the initiative and moving towards us in our humanity and need. They are tangible, perceivable evidences of an intangible reality: that God loves us and that Love has not only a heart, but hands and feet and a voice as well. The bread and the wine of the Lord's Supper are a solemn pledge of God's mercy and forgiveness offered to the sinner on the grounds of Christ's death. The personal receiving of these emblems simply emphasises this thrilling truth that God loves me as if I were the only one in all the world to be loved.

Hans Kung summarises the central importance of this meal for the Christian church:

> So much is clear: the Lord's Supper is the centre of the church and of its various acts of worship. Here the church is truly itself, because it is wholly with its Lord; here the church of Christ is gathered for its most intimate fellowship, as sharers in a meal. In this fellowship they draw strength for their service in the world. Because this meal is a meal of recollection and thanksgiving, the church is essentially a community which remembers and thanks. And because this meal is a meal of covenant and fellowship, the church is essentially a community which loves without ceasing. And because finally this meal is an anticipation of the eschatalogical meal, the church is essentially a community which looks to the future with confidence. Essentially, therefore, the church must be a meal-fellowship, a *koinonia* or *communio*; it must be a fellowship with Christ and with Christians, or it is not the church of Christ. In the Lord's Supper it is stated with incomparable clarity that the church is the *ecclesia*, the congregation, the community of God.

Often it is when we come together at the Lord's Supper as the body of Christ on earth, in Calvary love and fellowship with the Lord and with one another, that there is an eager expectation that Christ will move among us in power. There is a spiritual dynamic released when true divine fellowship is combined with true human fellowship secured at the cross. There is a new tenderness and openness towards one another and a willingness to discover what it really means to love one another as Christ loves us, and lay down our lives for one another. In the communion service in our church we have seen unbelievers brought to faith in Jesus Christ as they witness the reality amongst us. Others are convicted of sin as Spirit and sacrament unite with the word in the powerful presentation of the heart of God in grace and forgiveness. So many people struggle with a sense of unworthiness on the one hand and a proud and stubborn heart on the other, making forgiveness difficult to receive and also equally difficult to give. As the heart of the gospel is laid bare in the breaking of the bread and the pouring out of the wine, so hearts are melted in the awareness of the selfless giving of the sinless Son of God, the just for the unjust, that we might be free. It is especially appropriate to minister to the sick within this service and I have found, frequently, that quite specific answers to prayer are given.

On the grounds of Christ's finished work on the cross, together with his resurrection, ascension and the outpouring of the Holy Spirit, he stretches out his hands to us, in the Lord's Supper, in his love: 'Come, for all is now ready.'

I cannot conceive of thinking about forgiveness without drawing attention to this wonderful provision of God, commanded by his Son, to meet him at his table. My heart never fails to stir as I enter myself, and lead others towards, the great moment of receiving bread and wine with the words of the prayer of penitence:

Almighty God, our Heavenly Father,
we have sinned against you and against our fellow
    men,
in thought and word and deed,
through negligence, through weakness,
through our own deliberate fault.

We are truly sorry,
and repent of all our sins.
For the sake of your Son Jesus Christ, who died for
us,
Forgive us all that is past;
and grant that we may serve you in newness of life
to the glory of your name. Amen.

Almighty God
who forgives all who truly repent,
have mercy upon us,
pardon and deliver us from all our sins,
confirm and strengthen us in all goodness,
and keep us in life eternal;
through Jesus Christ our Lord. Amen.

8

The forgotten Father

Forgiveness, in the final analysis, is not dependent on technique or feelings, longings or obligations; it is a matter of realising the nature of God. Forgiveness fails because our understanding of God is faulty. So often God – even in Christian hearts – has little more reality than Santa Claus or the tooth-fairy. We would, of course, contest this, but when real life is tough we do not respond or react in a way that unequivocally demonstrates that we believe in 'God the Father Almighty, maker of heaven and earth'; the God and Father of our Lord Jesus Christ; the God who has taken the initiative to reveal what he is really like through his creation, in his Son, and in the Bible. Our reactions reveal that although what we say we believe seems certain enough, our trust in God is way behind.

It is hard for us to grasp that God is real. He does not have a body like ours – although he has a mind, a heart, and a will, and is a person. Our struggle with reality about God is compounded by the fact that he never has had, nor will ever have, a birthday. So God is outside the dimensions of space and time in which we live. Reality, for us, is always contained within these dimensions: but

God is beyond them. When we discover, in addition, that there are no limits to what he knows, how he can act, and where he is, we find ourselves really struggling to come to terms with reality! God is so totally 'other' and different from us that we are hard-pushed to come to terms with him. God is as much at home in the realm of the impossible as he is in the realm of the possible. Astonishingly, the Bible assures us that he made everything. There is nothing within creation that he has not brought into being. Furthermore, the Old Testament categorically indicates that he made everything out of nothing.

Equally astonishing is the Bible's assertion that God made everything for man. God's intention is that man should subdue the things that God has made and use them for God's own purposes. When God made the world it was good. If anything is bad, it is not because he created it so or intended it to be that way. Something has gone wrong; since when it left the heart of God it was all right. The car that I drive has given me very little trouble although I have already driven it over forty thousand miles. When it left the factory it was passed as being in good order. If, however, I abuse it in the way I drive it, or neglect to have it properly serviced, I should not be surprised if it no longer functions as the maker intended, nor should I blame the manufacturer.

So it is with God – he created perfection and gave instructions for good performance, but we have spoiled what he has given us and abused our freedom and control in using it.

In all of this we need to grasp the true nature of God. He demands truth, yet he deals with us in grace; he upholds perfect justice, and yet he is merciful to us; he loathes sin, and yet he loves the sinner; he is cleaner than we can ever imagine, and yet he was prepared to get his hands dirty by coming to live amongst us. His power is always motivated by his love, and his love is always backed up by his power. His judgment is sure (although he does not send in his bills every Friday), and yet his mercy is infinite. He does not turn a blind eye to our wrong-doing, and yet his attitude towards us is forever tender. It is so easy to emphasise his grace and love and mercy, and to lose sight of his holiness and anger and judgment. We must preserve both aspects of God's nature in equal balance. To do otherwise is to lack honesty and integrity and to have a false view of the God with whom we have to do.

Grace

Running through the Bible from beginning to end is the revelation of God as a God of grace. It is as true of the Old Testament as it is of the New Testament. Paul begins and ends every one of his letters contained there with a reference to God's grace. For Paul this is the very essence of what it means to be a Christian. For him, as for us, religion that centres on our own effort is futile to secure a living relationship with God. Our only hope is that God is what he has revealed himself to be – a God of grace.

Grace is one of those familiar words with an elusive meaning. It originally meant physical beauty, attractive-ness and social charm. It means a winsome and lovely quality. When referring to God's nature the word 'grace' signifies the sheer undeserved generosity of his heart. There are some Christian words that have a strong note of severity about them – but not this one. As we realise the abundance of God's grace, all we can do is receive what he is offering with adoring, wondering and grateful hearts.

To speak of someone being gracious can convey the idea of something passive. To speak of God's grace, how-ever, is to speak of a God who actively cares and goes on caring for someone who is completely unworthy and entirely undeserving. Grace and merit are mutually exclusive. A good example of this in the Old Testament comes powerfully out of the prophecy of Hosea. A subtitle for that prophecy could well be 'The Prophet and the Prostitute'. When Hosea, the prophet, married his wife the event hit the headlines. Everyone knew what he was; and at the same time, everyone knew what *she* was. To everyone it seemed crazy. What the gossips predicted came true. She soon ran away with another man. She had a child that was not Hosea's. He searched the streets for her until he found her. When he found her he did not recognise her because of the effects of her immoral and dissolute lifestyle. He brought her back home to love her tenderly and care for her generously. Through this experience he preached that God cares. Through his heart-break and frustration and bewilderment he was able with depth and insight to declare that God is like this. God's people, Israel, had been an unfruitful and unfaithful wife to God – but God pursued her because he cared for her. Such is the clear revelation of God in the Old Testament.

In the New Testament the emphasis is not different. In Luke 6 Jesus says simply of God: 'For he is good to the ungrateful and the wicked . . .' The apostle Paul cries, 'For we ourselves were once foolish, disobedient and wrong. We were slaves to passions and pleasures of all kinds. We spent our lives in malice and envy; others hated us and we hated them.' (In other words we used to be in a real mess!) 'But', he goes on, 'when the kindness and love of God our Saviour was revealed, he saved us. It was not because of any good deeds that we ourselves had done, but because of his own mercy that he saved us, through the Holy Spirit, who gives us new birth and new life by washing us. God poured out the Holy Spirit abundantly on us through Jesus Christ our Saviour, so that by his grace we might be put right with God and come into possession of the eternal life we hope for' (Titus 3:3–7). This is grace – positive, active, creative.

The incarnation
We can never know how much God cares until we look

at Jesus – until we see, first of all, that he was willing to leave the glory and perfection of heaven and come and live among us. This lies at the heart of the Christian message: God cared enough to become man and live where we do. Noel Richards has so movingly encapsulated the remarkable wonder of this in the words:

> You laid aside Your majesty, gave up everything for me,
> suffer'd at the hands of those You had created.
> You took all my guilt and shame,
> When You died and rose again . . .

Just so. He came from the glory of heaven and was born in a dirty stable enclosure under the stars, where we would never choose to see babies born. Such is the nature of grace in the heart of God – he came among us and lived here.

God's power

We see the grace of God, too, when we realise how he uses his power. Power is a neutral thing. It can heal or hurt, it can create or destroy – it all depends on who is using it. Mankind today is no stranger to the reality of power. The atomic bomb dropped on Hiroshima in 1945 killed over 75,000 people instantly. Seven years later the first hydrogen bomb was tested, and that was 1,000 times more powerful than the first atomic bomb. I understand that there is an explosive potential in our world today which is the equivalent of ten tons of TNT for every man, woman and child!

Although we often abuse power in order to oppress or control, God, in Jesus, used his power to heal the sick, release those who were in demonic captivity and raise the dead. His power was used to feed the hungry and banish raw terror in some fishermen's hearts when they were convinced that they would never make land again. Such is the consistent record of the gospels. God's power was used to create and not to destroy. He uses it positively and not negatively, bringing hope and not despair. God uses his power for good and not for evil, bringing life rather than death.

God never gives up

Perhaps nowhere is the grace of God more demonstrated in human lives than in his persistence with us. I have already referred to this incident, but I can remember vividly my own deep anger at God when my mother died after a two-year losing battle with cancer. It was not only her death which distressed me, but the way in which she died. It was so horrendous, humiliating, and cruel. In the months which followed her death, my home disintegrated as my brother married and my father remarried. Loneliness intensified my grief and both fuelled my anger – but God persisted. During my undergraduate years at Glasgow University reading philosophy and history, my immature and badly-founded faith was seriously questioned. Many of my ideas were wildly assaulted by the intellectualism which I absorbed during those years. The faith of my fathers seemed so naive, simplistic and improbable. Doubts about the divinity of Christ, the authority of scripture and the relevance of the church, and a dozen other fundamental 'convictions' that I had been brought up to affirm assailed me like a great barrage of mental and emotional artillery – but God persisted. Out of all this confusion God affirmed his call of me to the ordained ministry. This was to be authenticated by a little church in a back street of an industrial town in the west of Scotland. I still feel my face redden with shame as I recall the infantile pride of my heart at resisting such an invitation – for I had so very little to offer and that congregation was so very, very gracious. Pride caused me to reject their initial approaches to me (how grateful I am today that they did not give up!) – but God persisted.

As the years passed I left the west of Scotland and went to be a pastor in a thriving, busy church just north of Edinburgh. It was a congregation of some reputation and

I wanted to do much there. I worked hard from morning till night, often with no respite on any given week, and was in danger of neglecting my family, the needs of my own heart, and fellowship with God – but God persisted. In the late 'sixties I arrived at my present pastorate having learned so much from both my previous ones and very quickly found myself feeling lonely in both life and ministry. The healing and deliverance ministries were not developed (or even recognised!) in the church and Anne and I found ourselves increasingly involved in both. I had no pastoral help in those days and the leadership was divided anyway. How could I possibly maintain the ongoing life of the fellowship to which I had been called and at the same time develop ministries that God seemed to be thrusting upon us whilst caring for the needs of my family and maintaining spiritual freshness in my own spiritual life? I became very critical of God for putting me in such an impossible position. The whole thing was compounded by the fact that Jesus had baptised both Anne and me in the Holy Spirit only months before we arrived here, and I was desperately trying to work all this out theologically and experimentally in my own life and in the life of the fellowship! What was I to do? I was highly critical of God – but God persisted.

In more recent days I have struggled with my changing role in ministry. At heart and by preference I am a pastor, yet God has widened the horizons for ministry both nationally and internationally and has given unmistakable encouragement to develop a wider ministry. I have no doubt about the nature of his calling on my life in these years, but that does not make it any easier to come to terms with it, or to live with it. I thank God that I am part of a fellowship which is so wonderfully supportive and encouraging and that has been affirming and generous to a fault. That has not totally eliminated my personal struggle and resulting criticism of God – but God has persisted.

As I am writing it is only ten days ago, while I was in

the middle of a conference in Switzerland, that God met me powerfully again. I am sure beyond any shadow of a doubt that God, who has so valiantly persisted with me, is the God of grace with whom we have to do. God goes on and on out of the sheer generosity of his heart and does not give up on us. This is grace. This is God. This is how God cares.

God died for us

In its fullest measure God's grace is seen in the death of his Son on the cross. Liberal theology has constantly emphasised that the cross is the supreme evidence of how much God loves us. Evangelical theology emphasises that the cross is the unique and satisfactory way that a holy God can and does rescue and redeem sinful mankind. Christianity in its biblical form requires that the cross does both – it not only redeems man, but it also reveals God. Through the centuries we have always looked back to that dramatic event at the heart of history where God-made-flesh hung on a Roman gibbet and died and the church has consistently said: 'This is what God is like.' He died not only for the good but for the bad. He died not only for his friends, but for those who were hostile to him. The apostle Paul, in helping us understand the gospel, says, in Romans 8. 'God . . . who did not even keep back his own Son, but offered him up for us all! He gave us his Son – will he not also freely give us all things?' This is the God with whom we have to do. This is the God in whom and through whom forgiveness becomes a liberating reality.

He gives us his Spirit

There is yet one more evidence of God's grace. Before Jesus finally left his disciples he assured them, 'When I go, you will not be left alone . . .' He was stressing to them in their distress, 'I have other plans to take care of you when I am away from you.' He was, of course, referring to the ministry of his Holy Spirit. The last weekend of Jesus' 'earthly' life occupies about half of the gospel of John – and twenty-five per cent of the fourth gospel is devoted to the night before Jesus died on the cross. Jesus spent a good deal of that last night giving his disciples urgent instructions for their development, service and survival after he had gone. Many of these instructions refer to the person and ministry of the Holy Spirit.

Jesus has now returned to the place from whence he came, taking with him his human nature and experience. He has ensured, however, that his place on earth has been taken over by the Holy Spirit who has no body but lives in Christians. So his new body on earth, the church, is able to function in a divine dimension; dependent on God and giving honour and glory to the Father and the Son in the power of his Spirit. No wonder Melody Green can sing with such joy and gratitude:

Thank you, O my Father, for giving us Your Son,
and leaving Your Spirit till
the work on earth is done!

God is too concerned for our frail humanity to abandon us and leave us like orphans – vulnerable and frustrated. Thank God that in his grace he sends his Spirit!

God loves us

How clearly we need to grasp the nature of God if we are ever going to enter into the reality and joy of being forgiven and forgiving! To all that we know of God's grace, God's love is added. In fact it is always God's loving which lies behind his caring. Love has become such an abused word within our society that it now covers a whole range of reactions, activities, attitudes and responses: some of them reprehensible and destructive rather than honourable and creative. It is so easy to have an understanding of love which is sentimental rather than scriptural.

The Bible speaks of four directions which the love of God takes. First is God's love for his own Son. Before anything was created, before there was an earth or a universe – God loved because God is love. There were loving persons within the Godhead of Father, Son and Holy Spirit. I cannot grasp this fully, but I do realise that if you affirm that God is love you need to assume the Trinity. The very first love that God ever had – stretching backwards and forwards into eternity – was for his own Son. It is always moving to see a father's love for his son – but we have never really seen the magnificence of the father/son relationship until we have seen the love of our heavenly Father and his heavenly Son.

Jesus was always talking about this in the gospels. Amidst all the hostility he encountered this one thing remained constant – God loved him. This is what made his baptism such a thrilling experience – for as he stood praying, after his baptism, heaven opened and God spoke: 'This is my own beloved Son.' Later Jesus declared with unaffected confidence, 'The Father loves the Son and shows him what he is doing.' Still later as he comforted his disciples when they were feeling insecure and apprehensive about the future he said, 'As the Father loves me, so I love you.' 'That is the nature and quality of my love for you!' He was God's first love.

God loves the Jews
But the Bible also affirms God's love for the Jews. This is perhaps the most extraordinary reality in the whole of history. Few have shown compassion towards the Jews. On the contrary they have been widely criticised and universally disliked. Yet God loves the Jews.

Why is this so? God tells them, 'From all the peoples on earth the Lord your God chose you to be his own special people. The Lord did not love you and choose you because you outnumbered other peoples; you were the smallest nation on earth. But the Lord loved you . . .' (Deuteronomy 7:6–8). In other words it was not because there was anything *in* the Jews that made God love them. We are constantly looking for something in the beloved that stimulates God's love. However closely we look we can never find anything. God loves me not because there is anything attractive or loveable in me, but simply because he loves me. We constantly try to find the reason for God's love in us and we cannot. The reason for God's love is in *him* and not in us. This has been powerfully demonstrated in God's love for the Jews. It is natural for us to ask, 'What do the Jews have that others do not have?' It is not because they are religious or superior or worthy or attractive or significant that God loves them. This brings remarkable security not only to them, but to us – and to me. God loves me because God loves me. I cannot understand it; I find it hard to believe it – but it is true. I can never fully enter into the wonder of forgiveness until I begin to touch this reality about God.

God loves the world
The third direction which the love of God takes is his love for his world. As I stand on the crowded concourse of Euston station and watch hundreds and hundreds of people rushing around on a summer Saturday I struggle as I say to myself, 'God knows every one of these people and loves them all.' How on earth can this be so? I can love a number of people after a fashion, but the number I can love personally and really significantly is very few. And I have a constant tendency to reduce God to my size. I view God, so often, in the light of my own experience and ability. If I am unable to grasp a love so vast then I automatically infer that it cannot be that vast. Yet God is God, and his love is so vast that he can significantly embrace millions; past and future as well as present. 'God loved the world so much', the Bible cries, 'that he gave his only Son, so that everyone who believes in him may not die, but have eternal life.' I can only accept this by faith and release its reality in my own experience as I confront every fault and failure and imperfection with a stubborn statement of that faith: 'Nevertheless God loves me.' He said so! I believe it! That settles it for me!

God loves me

It would be so easy for me to be swallowed up in the general wonder of the reality that God loves the world. It would be so easy to lose sight of the fourth direction of God's love – and that is God's love for the individual. 'The Son of God loved me', cries Saul the persecutor become Paul the preacher, 'and gave himself for me.' He might well have added, 'And that's the end of it.' Some of us need a huge injection of this reality in order to blast us out of our low self-image. I can truthfully say, 'I am loved by God.' This is fact and not fantasy. This is truth and not error. One of the greatest theologians since the apostle Paul was Augustine. He had his own intense struggles and lost the battle many a time. However, he discovered what he declared, 'God loves everyone of us as if there were only one of us to love.' he knows my name; he knows my need; he knows my nature – and he loves me. Even with my Scottish reserve and my stubborn self-will and my monumental failures, he loves me. It is not sugary sentimentality, it is reality. It is not a passive concept, it is a pursuing conquest. The SAS may well have the motto 'Who Dares Wins', but God's motto must surely be 'Who Loves Conquers' – if we will respond to that love and receive it.

This is what God is all about. This is what his love is all about. This is what forgiveness is all about. I have never come across a love like this anywhere else, but love like this is in God and from God. This is what undergirds forgiveness and forgiving. This is the dimension God wants to bring us into in the power of his Holy Spirit. Man can and does lay down his life for his friend (occasionally), but God laid down his life for his enemies. Man can and does lay down his life for those whom he loves, but God laid down his life for those who hated him. As a boiling volcano reveals the fire that always burns at the core of the earth, so the cross of Calvary reveals the love that burns eternally at the core of God. And this reality remains forever the same. Our senses and experience do not enable us to grasp this, but the Holy Spirit wants to enable us.

God's mercy

One more thing needs to be said about the nature and character of God to finalise the reality of our forgiveness. It is that God is a God of mercy. Mercy is the opposite of justice, since justice is what I deserve whilst mercy is what I do not deserve.

A lady went once to have her photograph taken by a professional photographer in his studio. She had prepared as well as she knew how to – hairdo, cosmetics, choice of clothes and jewelry. He was set up as competently as he always was – lighting, back-drop, cameras, assistant. The photographs were taken and the deposit given. 'I hope these photographs will do me justice!' she said, somewhat pretentiously and pompously. When she had gone out of earshot the photographer said, 'Madam, it is not justice you need, it is mercy!' Just so!

When Jesus was among us he was persistently concerned to make sure that we understood fully that God is a God of mercy. Perhaps his best-known illustration of the mercy of God was the story of the Good Samaritan. Often this story has been portrayed, wrongly, as a good deed story – an exercise in spiritual Boy Scouting. It is a mercy story. There has never been a deeper divide in human relationships than that which existed between the Jews and the Samaritans. The Samaritan saw a bleeding, helpless, mugged Jew – a man who would despise him – lying in a ditch. He went out of his way to care for this man at personal risk and cost. This is not a 'good deed' story, it is a 'mercy' story. Mercy is a quality demonstrated to the undeserving when all right to a favourable responses has been quite legitimately forfeited.

So it is with God. By right and by choice, all we can rightly expect is justice; but God extends his mercy to us. No wonder Charles Wesley sang with such conviction:

'Tis mercy all, immense and free;

For, O my God, it found me out!

No condemnation now I dread;
Jesus, and all in him, is mine!
Alive in Him, my living Head,
And clothed in righteousness divine.
Bold I approach the eternal throne
and claim the crown, through Christ, my own.

Whatever my shame and failure, my hope rises as I grasp
the reality of God's mercy 'immense and free'. However
much I might despise myself and feel condemned by
others, I am forgiven and free because God is a God of
mercy. How often I have come to this in my own life!
How often I have seen the miracle of forgiveness itself in
freedom in the lives of others, as they too have grasped
the reality of the mercy of God.

Jesus affirmed that the only people who will really be
blessed as they come to worship before God are those
who rely upon God's mercy. I once heard a story which
struck me, initially, as over-sentimental, but I have since
discovered that it has the merit of being true. A little girl
was born into a devout Christian home in England. There
she grew up in love and security. Her parents were neither
indulgent nor irresponsible – although they no doubt
made many mistakes as all parents do. Her home was
comfortable and welcoming and the garden in which she
often played, alone and with her friends, ran down to a
fence which protected it from the main north-south railway line which ran all the way to London.

At the bottom of the garden, overlooking the railway
line, was an apple tree. She and her friends often climbed
into the tree and waved to crew and passengers as they
thundered past on their way to and from London. (This
was still the age of the steam-train and people seemed to
want to do that then!)

As she grew up she began to be very critical of her
parents. Tension and bad feeling crept into that home.

Nothing that the parents did seemed to alleviate or alter the situation. Criticism turned to hostility and soon it seemed that nothing could please or satisfy her – even the simple expressions of their love for her caused explosive irritation.

Eventually she decided that she did not want them to be part of her life. She wanted her freedom and to their bewilderment and heart-break went to London. Contact with her was difficult and became non-existent. She found freedom a hard task-master. To be free to do entirely what you like and want brought enormous pressure and unbelievable captivity. She made choices that were foolish, immature and wrong. Life became very complicated and confused. Relationships were superficial and soon ended; habits took root and became impossible to break; money was hard to come by honestly, and sheer survival became the target, rather than living. Determination made her stick at it and remain beholden to none.

Physically shattered, morally messed up, mentally in darkness, and spiritually dead she went to the Embankment one night, intent on ending it all in the River Thames. As she stood there on the edge of suicide and the unknown she thought of her home – again. Although still only in her early twenties she had lost touch completely. Were her parents still alive? Did they still live where they had always lived? Had her behaviour and attitude towards them destroyed the love that had so obviously been there and had been so often and so tenderly expressed? Quite irrationally (or was it that two people never stopped praying for her?) she decided that she would try one more route to freedom. She would write home and tell them the whole sordid story in the hope that in spite of everything they might have her back and the future could be put together somehow.

Fears and doubts tumbled over one another as she pursued this thought a bit more. Had her parents at last given up on her? Had they become occupied in some other way so that their lives were now full of other things and there was no space left for her? Had long-remembered tenderness given way to hardness and bitterness? Has justice finally taken the place of mercy? However, write she did. To ensure that they would not be embarrassed by her request to come home she thought of a plan that would be least awkward for all concerned. 'If you'll have me back', she wrote, 'I will come on a train from London. If I am welcome to come home hang something white on the apple tree at the bottom of the garden. I realise that I have no longer any right to expect you to have me, and so if the apple tree has nothing white on it I will understand.'

She made the journey north from London. As she approached familiar territory she hardly dared to look out of the railway-carriage window. As she passed the bottom of the garden she saw the apple tree ablaze with white – sheets, pillow-cases, table-cloths, handkerchiefs!

This is mercy! This is God!

9

And finally . . .

The middle walk of the public park in Dunfermline was the location for many of my exertions. It was there that I taught both my older children to ride a bike. As yet I had no concept of the pints of adrenalin that would be dumped into my cardio-vascular system as I taught them how to drive a car! I thought then that getting them to stay upright on a bicycle was demanding enough, as I raced breathlessly alongside them holding on to the back of the saddle. At some point, unable to keep up the pace, I had to let them go. As I watched them wobble their insecure way into the distance I realised there was another problem to be faced – they did not know how to stop satisfactorily.

Bitterness and resentment bring feelings which put us on that course – they carry us around and around the same senseless circle. They carry us around and around ourselves. Can't someone do something which will grab hold of the handlebars and break into our lives to deliver us and enable us to stop and begin again? Only forgiveness can do that for us. Only forgiveness can break in and interrupt our endless orbiting around ourselves and set us free. The Bible describes it in this way:

> Get rid of all bitterness, passion and anger. No more
> shoutings or insults, no more hateful feelings of any
> sort. Instead, be kind and tender-hearted to one
> another, and forgive one another as God has forgiven
> you through Christ (Ephesians 4:31 and 32).

Only the kind of forgiveness God showed us in Jesus Christ
can sweeten our bitterness and bring tender-hearted
healing. As we have thought our way through forgiveness – both received and given – we need now to do
something about it. Reach out and receive it from God
who wants to give it; release it now, immediately, to those
who need our forgiveness. This is not just because this is
the safest way for your own self-hood and sanity, but for
a much deeper reason – it is the way of Christ.

Jesus' way was the way of giving forgiveness even
before it was asked, and even when it was not and never
would be asked by others. To imagine that we need not
forgive until we are asked to do so needs to be challenged
and dealt with. Forgive immediately, now! And then –
forgive continually. Make forgiveness a way of life – constantly and consistently and completely. Forgiveness is
not leaving a person with the burden of 'something to live
down'; it is offering him someone to live with! A friend
like you.

The greatest test of continual forgiveness is the daily
kind of forgiving love which gives and takes, freely accept-
ing the bruises and hurts of living. This is supernatural –
it is certainly not natural. But then, are we not supposed
to be living a naturally supernatural life and a supernatu-
rally natural life? Here is the opportunity to prove that it
is real, and it works.

> Love is not ill-mannered or selfish or irritable; love
> does not keep a record of wrongs; love is not happy
> with evil, but is happy with the truth. Love never
> gives up; and its faith, hope and patience never fail.
> Love is eternal (1 Corinthians 13:5–8).

The past is the past. Nothing can alter the facts. What has happened has happened forever. But the meaning can be changed – that is *forgiveness*.

Forgiveness releases us from our captivity to the past, restores the present, and heals for the future.

Forgiveness is acceptance with no exception. It accepts not only the hurt you have received, it also accepts the one who did the hurting, and it accepts the loss caused by the hurtful actions and words.

Forgiveness is self-giving with no self-seeking. It gives love where the enemy expects hatred. It gives freedom where the enemy deserves punishment. It gives understanding where the enemy anticipates anger and revenge. Forgiveness refuses to seek its own advantage. It gives back to the other person his freedom and his future.

Never am I more fully human than when I forgive – for never am I more fully like Jesus, and this is our calling as Christians. This is how God deals with us, and he calls us to do the same to others. So new life will flow to our withered hearts; new energy to our paralysed emotions; and new understanding to our frozen feelings. Thank God for forgiveness!